NO FAMILY IS AN ISLAND

EXPERTISE

**CULTURES AND
TECHNOLOGIES
OF KNOWLEDGE**

EDITED BY DOMINIC BOYER

*A list of titles in this series is available
at www.cornellpress.cornell.edu.*

No Family Is an Island

Cultural Expertise among Samoans in Diaspora

Ilana Gershon

Cornell University Press
Ithaca and London

First published 2012 by Cornell University Press
First printing, Cornell Paperbacks, 2012
Printed in the United States of America

Library of Congress Cataloging-in-Publication Data

Gershon, Ilana.
    No family is an island : cultural expertise among Samoans in diaspora /
Ilana Gershon.
        p. cm. — (Expertise)
    Includes bibliographical references and index.
    ISBN 978-0-8014-5078-5 (cloth : alk. paper)
    ISBN 978-0-8014-7805-5 (pbk. : alk. paper)
    1. Samoan Americans—California—Social conditions.   2. Samoans—
New Zealand—Social conditions.   3. Samoa—Emigration and
immigration—Social aspects.   4. California—Emigration and
immigration—Social aspects.   5. New Zealand—Emigration
and immigration—Social aspects.   I. Title.   II. Series: Expertise
(Ithaca, N.Y.)
    F870.S17G47   2012
    305.89'9462—dc23   2011046583

Cornell University Press strives to use environmentally responsible sup-
pliers and materials to the fullest extent possible in the publishing of its
books. Such materials include vegetable-based, low-VOC inks and acid-
free papers that are recycled, totally chlorine-free, or partly composed of
nonwood fibers. For further information, visit our website at
www.cornellpress.cornell.edu.

Cloth printing   10 9 8 7 6 5 4 3 2 1
Paperback printing   10 9 8 7 6 5 4 3 2 1

For Solo Collins

Contents

Acknowledgments

When I look at the pages of this book, I see the traces of other people's patience. Penny Schoeffel, Malama Meleisea, Judith Huntsman, and Helen Tuitama gently suggested less cumbersome ways to think about other people's actions. Solo Collins as well as her friends and family talked to me for hours and hours about what it means to care for others in a Samoan family. Trish Epati brought such good humor and common sense to bear, along with Semi, Tiana, and Mana Epati. Many wise people told me stories about how to work alongside government bureaucracies, or how to manage the oddities of living a moral Samoan life among oblivious capitalist people: Joann Below, Fia Carlos-Valentino, Tom Church, Lyneki, Fofoa, Rev. Risatisone and Fereni Ete, Toeutu Fa'aleava, Fatilua Fatilua, Marilyn Kohlhase, Pat Luce, Lealaisalanoa Setu Petaia, Sam Ripley, Rev. Ioritana and Lonise Tanielu, Tina Tuitama, and Dee Uhile. Some of the people who were the most patient and generous I wish to keep anonymous. They shared the stories of their lives with me and did not necessarily anticipate the ways I would interweave these stories into an academic discussion of being cultural or acultural.

I have learned through the many years of writing and revising this book how many debts a single manuscript can incur. Several people read the whole draft and gave me helpful insights as to how to fix what still feels like a myriad of problems, fewer after people's careful editing: Amy Cohen, Nina Eliasoph, Jane Goodman, Matt Tomlinson, and Peter Wissoker. Cornell University Press found incredible anonymous reviewers, reviewers that dramatically improved the book. People also read various drafts of different chapters or talked to me at length about ideas: Richard Bauman, Melissa Demian, Matthew Engelke, J. Joseph Errington, Henry Goldschmidt, Carol Greenhouse, Nancy Jacobs, Michael Kral, Anne Lorimer, Ray McDermott, Phil Parnell, Dhooleka Sarhadi Raj, James Rizzo, Paitra Russell, Paul Ryer, Karen Schiff, Michael W. Scott, Kimbra Smith, Janelle Taylor, Herve Varenne, and Zolani Ngwane.

A warm network of academics who work on Samoan issues or the Pacific in general also were very influential: Joan Ablon, Ping-Ann Addo, Melani Anae, Niko Besnier, Alessandro Duranti, Michael Goldsmith, Phyllis Herda, J. Kehaulani Kauanui, Heather Young-Leslie, Cluny MacPherson, John Mayer, Mark Mosko, Julie Park, Paul Shankman, Bradd Shore, and Unasa Va'a. My department here at Indiana University was generous in its support, and I am grateful to all my colleagues. Faculty at University of Chicago encouraged me throughout my long fieldwork and the first moments of writing about Samoan migrants, although this manuscript must look foreign to them by now: my dissertation advisor John Kelly as well as Homi Bhabha, Susan Gal, Nancy Munn, and Marshall Sahlins. I owe a special debt of gratitude to my MA supervisor, Marilyn Strathern, whose imprint is on every page, refracted through my ethnographic material and my idiosyncratic interpretations.

Several chapters have originated as articles: "Compelling Culture: The Rhetoric of Assimilation among Samoan Migrants in the United States," *Ethnic and Racial Studies* 30 (2007): 787–816; "When Culture Is Not a System: Why Samoan Cultural Brokers Can Not Do Their Job," *Ethnos* 71 (2006): 533–558; "Converting Meanings and the Conversion of Meaning in Samoan Moral Economies," in *The Limits of Meaning,* edited by Matt Tomlinson and Matthew Engelke, 147–164 (Berghahn Press, 2006); "Becoming Minor Minorities in the United States and New Zealand: Samoan

Migrant Experiences with Government Funding," in *Selected Papers on Refugees and Immigrants* (9), edited by MaryCarol Hopkins and Nancy Wellmeier (American Anthropological Association, 2001); "Going Nuclear: New Zealand Bureaucratic Fantasies of Samoan Extended Families" in *New Directions in Anthropological Kinship,* edited by Linda Stone, 303–321 (Rowman and Littlefield Publishers, 2001); and "How to Know When Not to Know: Strategic Ignorance When Eliciting for Samoan Migrant Exchanges," *Social Analysis* 44(2000): 84–105.

Writing a book is never just about the writing. Debbora Battaglia, Fran Benson, Jane Fajans, Peter Potter, and Joel Robbins provided invaluable support when I found the manuscript itself too daunting and unwieldy. Amy Cohen, Melissa Demian, Jane Goodman, Nancy Lightfoot, and Teri Silvio gave me intellectual and emotional encouragement throughout the many years.

I want to thank the Wenner-Gren Foundation, the National Science Foundation, the Spencer Foundation, and the Social Science Research Council's Migration Program for supporting the fieldwork.

Finally, I want to thank my mother, Paula Girshick, whose steadfast support helped me through many drafts. And David Fisher, who learned early on to say, "Oh no, not the Samoan book" and only meant it 37.2 percent of the time.

No Family Is an Island

INTRODUCTION

By the time I started writing drafts of grant proposals for the National Office of Samoan Affairs in California, I thought I had a fairly good sense of how to present Samoan culture to granting agencies. I had spent the previous year and a half in New Zealand (1996–1997), studying how Samoan migrants managed government bureaucracies there. But it turns out that I kept getting it all wrong. The more experienced grant writers in the head office in California changed all of my sentences; they didn't think my points would be persuasive to granting agencies.

One critical mistake I made was to overestimate the significance of culture in the eyes of U.S. government bureaucrats. In New Zealand, where I had volunteered at Samoan community-based organizations in Auckland and Wellington, the government's obligation to help preserve Samoan culture was widely assumed. In the United States, however, as I soon discovered, one could not make such an assumption. Thus, my early attempts to produce persuasive grant proposals on behalf of the Samoan community fell flat because I was making arguments for cultural support that were inappropriate in a U.S. context. The lesson I learned from my grant writing colleagues was a simple one: When presenting an ethnic group to U.S. government funders, discuss ethnicity in terms of race and class, not culture. Community-based Samoan organizations in the United States had learned this lesson the hard way, over the course of some forty odd years of back and forth with prospective funding agencies.

I didn't fully grasp the significance of this issue until I had a chance to read old grant applications from a now defunct Samoan organization, Samoa mo Samoa, submitted over a period of sixteen years, from 1979 to1995.[1] What these documents revealed was the trial and error process by which grant writers learned how to successfully present Samoans as a fundable ethnicity.[2] The organization was headed primarily by one woman, Nofoaluma Tuiasosopo, who did not feel comfortable writing grant applications herself; fortunately, therefore, she had a few people on staff who took the lead in writing them. All in all, I collected twenty-two grant proposals from Samoa mo Samoa, written during the organization's lifespan by a wide range of people, from lawyers to recent college graduates.

The first grant proposal I read, dating back to 1979, had been submitted to the United Way. In it the grant writers used explicitly assimilationist rhetoric to make the case for funding: The organization needed financial support to help Samoan migrants adjust to American culture. Interestingly enough, very little mention was made of Samoan culture. The writers used vague phrases such as "discipline is very stout and strict" or the "reverence and respectful nature of their culture" to discuss Samoan culture—but would go no further.[3] Moreover, the language used throughout the proposal implied that

---

1. Samoan Community Development Center, which was housing all of Samoa mo Samoa's papers, graciously allowed me to peruse all the files that remained. From other papers I found, it is clear that I did not find copies of all the grant proposals submitted, but I reviewed a good cross-section of successful and unsuccessful applications.

2. Samoa mo Samoa was founded in 1974. The earliest evidence of funding I uncovered was grants awarded by the San Francisco Foundation and San Francisco Comprehensive Employment and Training Act (CETA) program. Over the years Samoa mo Samoa received grants for a variety of other sources as well (none of them federal); e.g., Community Development Block Grant, Mayor's Office of Community Development, San Francisco Summer Youth Project, Peninsula Community Foundation, and the Vanguard Foundation. According to documents I found, these grants ranged from $400 to $44,000. The grant awarded for $44,000 was rescinded as a consequence of the Gramm-Rudman Act in 1985.

3. Of the twenty-two grants I collected, only one—for a youth center—discussed Samoan culture in any depth. The grant writers suggested that they would teach youth the kava ceremony,

Samoan migrants were unsophisticated and largely unfamiliar with American culture—as though American Samoa had not been an unincorporated U.S. territory since 1900 and contending with a U.S.–based education system since the 1950s. In one place the grant writers suggested that:

> A young life when migrated to the United States is taking a pivotal direction in exposing himself/herself to a completely strange environment. Here, positive actions are necessary and must be implemented quickly to reduce and prevent from being incapacitated by the ruinous current of problems that confront him or her.

Ultimately, the grant application was turned down. And for years after, new grant proposals were written, using much the same strategy. In some cases, they sounded similar to the drafts describing Samoans as an ethnic group like African Americans or Latinos; in others, they were closer to the grants describing Samoan culture I saw funded in New Zealand. Yet these applications all failed.

It took time, but eventually the grant writers for Samoa mo Samoa adjusted their approach. They learned that to be successful they had to present Samoans as a minority group, comparable with African American or Hispanic communities. A 1992 application for a Community Development program grant contains a typical example of this rhetoric, quoting an article published in the *San Francisco Examiner* in which Samoan students ages twelve through seventeen were shown to have the lowest test scores "of all the minorities in San Francisco." The grant writers had learned to present Samoans as an ethnic group whose distinctive features emerge from an amalgam of poverty and recent migration. In the United States, as opposed to New Zealand, Samoan organizations are fundable not because Samoan migrants might lose their culture but because they are at risk— just as other minorities are at risk.

In the broader world we live in today, culture is one of those key concepts that generates funding. Since the 1970s, government bureaucracies from Singapore to Sweden have gradually determined that a nation's cultural diversity requires bureaucratic support, ideally to create a level

---

how rituals to bestow a chiefly title were organized, and the principles of *ie toga* exchange (and used the term *ie toga* instead of the English equivalent, *fine mat*). The project was not funded.

playing field (Dusenbery 1997; Greenhouse 1998; Mackey 1999; Povinelli 2002). This often entails funding what the government defines as culture. But the definition of the culture that is being funded varies widely, as do the techniques for demonstrating that one has a culture suitable for funding. As I learned from my own experiences of grant writing in New Zealand and the United States, culture is not always funded in the same way or with the same goals in mind. What government bureaucracies will count as culture is determined primarily by the history of those bureaucracies and how the bureaucracies interact with each part of a country's multicultural population. Yet because culture, in these instances, is a result of classification (Bowker and Star 1999), what counts as culture is also being shaped by what doesn't count as culture. In the case of Samoan migrants navigating government bureaucracies in New Zealand and the United States, what this means is that they are navigating different ways of defining both the cultural and the acultural. At the same time, they are also acting upon their own definitions of what is cultural and acultural, developed in their local communities, churches, and among their extended families.

In this book, I examine this notion of the cultural and the acultural as it relates to Samoan migrants in the United States and New Zealand. In particular, I investigate how and when the cultural and the acultural become relevant for Samoan migrants as they encounter what they define as cultural differences in churches, ritual exchanges, welfare offices, and community-based organizations. In the first half of the book, I focus on how family members think about certain aspects of their lives as cultural moments and other aspects as acultural. In developing these divisions, they are responding to the changes in their daily lives that are due to the transnational circulation of people, money, and knowledge. Samoan migrant families will discuss what counts as cultural and acultural when thinking about instances of globalization in their lives. In the second half of the book, I look at how Samoan migrants manage their encounters with government officials, who have very different ideas of what counts as culture, who has it, and what it means to be a cultural expert.

The Cultural and the Acultural

When anthropologists think about *culture,* they usually frame it in terms of what is traditional and locatable (e.g., religious practices and family traditions). On the other hand, the *acultural* is typically framed as modern and universal (e.g., bureaucracies, laws, and technologies). In my own fieldwork, I found that Samoan migrants are quite skilled when it comes to distinguishing between what is cultural and what is acultural. In fact, culture was always contrasted with what was not cultural, but this comparison between the cultural and the acultural was often implicit. People talked easily to me about what practices were cultural, but they rarely described anything or anyone as acultural (although non-Samoan in-laws and misbehaving children could be an exception). I am looking at what one can learn about "culture" as a classificatory category when one examines the ways in which the cultural/acultural divide is constructed. What categories do my interlocutors in the field use when trying to make some differences visible and significant? How do people mutually constitute the "cultural" and "acultural" in different contexts and what are the consequences that flow from these constructions? How do different definitions and uses of the culture concept work when migrants are expected to be cultural experts in their dealings with state bureaucracies? Does the culture concept work in the same way when these migrants are invoking culture within their families or local communities?

For both Samoan migrants and government officials, the culture concept is tacitly accompanied by its classificatory opposite, the acultural. For example, for my interlocutors in the field, Samoan ritual exchanges are cultural whereas capitalist exchanges are not. This is not the case from an anthropological perspective, where all social interaction is cultural and there are no acultural moments, people, or spaces. But for those I met during fieldwork, the acultural haunts the cultural. And this often leads to essentializing culture and power inequalities (Briggs 2001; Handler 1988; Mackey 2002; Orta 2004; Santiago-Irizarry 1996; Taylor 2003).

Scholars of similar categorical divisions, such as whiteness or masculinity, tend to frame this distinction as a dichotomy between the marked and the unmarked (see Lakoff 2000). In much scholarly work, the acultural is hegemonic, normative, and naturalized (see Chock 1999; Urciuoli 1996; Yanagisako and Delaney 1995). In analyzing how ethnoscapes are constructed, Brackette Williams (1989) argues that dominant groups are positioned so that they are the only group supposedly unmarked by difference. Their practices—and thus their power—are naturalized. This was certainly at play in my fieldwork: Bureaucracies served to naturalize how systems operate, assuming that even families would organize themselves as though they were small bureaucratic systems.

Yet the impact of defining institutions or people as acultural goes well beyond the naturalization of power. In my fieldwork, the category of acultural also provided people with opportunities to disentangle from obligations and groups. This was in sharp contrast with how the culture category creates obligations and social unities. For example, a public Samoan family unity is performed when the bride's family brings together hundreds and hundreds of fine mats from family members scattered throughout Samoa, New Zealand, Australia, Hawaiʻi, and Utah. Bringing all the mats together was the result of long histories of cultural obligations and family affection. By contrast, exchanging "aculturally"—in this case, with capitalist principles, and focusing on one's households' needs instead of one's extended families—could undercut the work that went into forming these transnational familial unities. In other moments, being acultural is not antithetical to building social unities; for example, participating in an evangelical Christian church may be forming another community, one that is performed through activities other than public exchanges of money or fine mats. The perception of this form of Christianity as acultural contributes to perceptions that it creates timeless meaning. Or the acultural juxtaposed to the cultural allows people to act without reference to specific locations; that is, the acultural enables locationless practices. A-temporal, a-spatial, or a-social, strategies in an acultural vein can produce the possibilities for disconnection and disentanglement.

The acultural category is not only a way to classify arenas in which people can practice strategies of disentanglement. It also presents a creative space for imagining less predictable relationships to social orders. People have the chance to engage with what counts as tradition and expected behavior in less socially predictable ways when they can also call on a repertoire of putatively acultural practices. Practically speaking, Samoan migrants were able to form church communities in new ways, or raise their children with a mixture of techniques borrowed from New Zealand or U.S. media. In my fieldwork, the acultural also seemed to encompass social structures often categorized as modern: capitalism, welfare bureaucracies, and so on. The acultural often became synonymous with what is modern but, intriguingly, not inevitably.

When projected onto people in Samoan contexts, the acultural often became a way to frame people as out of place. But being out of place can also be liberating. When the cultural category becomes an explicit mode for classifying others' intentions and practices, the acultural can enable unanticipated (and unclassified) forms of social practice and analysis to emerge.

Culture in Hybrid Contexts

During my fieldwork I encountered a very particular kind of cultural hybridity among my interlocutors; that is, in any given context there was a good possibility that my interlocutors were negotiating multiple social orders, and these multiple social orders were jostling for relevance. This also meant that people could be engaging with multiple social orders simultaneously. As I discussed these issues with my interlocutors, they found culture to be a useful category to think with as they tried to understand the range of social strategies available to them. For them, navigating multiple social orders affected what it meant to be Samoan in practice; it often became essential for them to categorize particular contexts or social strategies explicitly as either cultural or acultural. They were often openly labeling people, practices, and situations as belonging to one form of social order (such as Samoan culture) and not to another (such as putatively acultural capitalism). In doing so, however, they couldn't just assign labels of cultural and acultural arbitrarily. They had to figure out how to classify and interact in a way that made sense to other Samoans.

By focusing on classification in contexts where multiple social orders are present, I am claiming that people's own reflexive engagement with their contexts is a crucial component for how and why people interact in the ways that they do. I am emphasizing people's own social analysis of situations to explain why certain miscommunications might arise between people who belong to different churches or different bureaucracies. This leads me to a crucial argument that runs throughout this book: The relationship between reflexivity and social orders is a dialogic one. People can have different reflexive, or analytical engagements, with social orders, while social orders also often require that people have particular reflexivities.[4] As a corollary, not all reflexivities are the same: the kind of reflexive social engagement required by a government bureaucracy is different from the kind of reflexive social engagement required by Samoan social order, as I discuss in chapter 3.

Historical Context

The experiences of Samoan migrants are particularly conducive for the kind of comparative analysis I undertake in this book because their historical relationships with both the United States and New Zealand have been so similar. For many years, New Zealand and the United States split control over these Pacific islands east of the International Date Line. The United States has governed American Samoa, the eastern part of this island group, since 1900. New Zealand gained Western Samoa (now independent Samoa) as a territory in 1914, taking over from Germany. In 1962, Western Samoa became independent, although it retained a special relationship with New Zealand. In both cases, these colonial ties provided people from Samoa with privileged status for immigration into the colonizing country, and since the 1950s people from Samoa have migrated to urban centers in increasing numbers. The total population of migrants has grown to 131,103 in New Zealand and 128,183 in the U.S. mainland and Hawai'i (New Zealand Census 2006; U.S. Census 2000). According to the New Zealand Census, 69 percent, or 48,147 Samoan adults have graduated from high school. In the United States, 59 percent of adult Samoans have a high school degree (Asian Pacific Islander American Health Forum [APIAHF] 2005).

In both countries, people from Samoa began migrating into complex ethnic constellations at the same time and with similar family patterns. However, over the past fifty years, the two governments' practices have ensured different types of political and economic experiences for Samoan migrants in each country. People from Samoa who live in New Zealand have access to a greater range of educational and employment opportunities

---

4. This may be an unfamiliar take on reflexivity in anthropology, where reflexivity often refers to the anthropologist's discussion of how their own subject position affects the ethnography (see Boyer, in press, for a historical overview of reflexivity in anthropology).

than those who live in the United States. Government policies have played an important role in fashioning this difference.

This difference in navigating bureaucracies does not have its origins in radically different colonial histories. Indeed, Samoan migrants learned similar strategies for how to protect their own interests under both the New Zealand and U.S. colonial administrations. Many of the Samoan community workers I met were from families that had developed expertise for years in dealing with New Zealand and U.S. bureaucracies. Under colonial indirect rule, Samoan leaders had honed their abilities to represent Samoan culture strategically. The policy of indirect rule created a space for people to choose how they wanted to represent Samoan political and social organization to the colonial powers in order to gain access to resources, both material and political. The colonial records are littered with descriptions of how colonial officials and Samoan chiefs frequently skirmished over where the exact boundaries of authority lay under an ill-defined commitment to indirect rule (Fa'aleava 2003; Meleisea 1987b).

A principal tension between the colonial government and the colonized was the disjuncture between an imposed bureaucracy geared toward centralization and an indigenous social organization premised on decentralization. The colonial bureaucracies frequently required one spokesman to represent Samoan custom or to be the authority over a designated area. In both Samoas, however, each village had a governing collective of chiefs who made all the decisions, tempered by the judicious intervention of the village church minister. While there were numerous ceremonial occasions when a pair of chiefs represented a district or an island, these were temporary (albeit possibly lifelong) moments in long drawn-out strategic maneuverings over rank. The colonial situation created the opportunity for some Samoan chiefs to represent themselves as the sole authority on Samoan custom (Meleisea 1987b). Migrants had grown up watching their elders evoking Samoan custom to resist colonial infringements as well as deploying it for their families' benefit within the intricacies of village politics. When people migrated from Samoa, the playing field for strategically evoking Samoan culture changed substantially. For example, migrants were no longer in contexts in which only they knew the indigenous political system and could thus gain certain concessions from the colonial officials.

Cluny Macpherson (1997) has outlined the three waves of Samoan migration that established Samoan communities in New Zealand. The pattern in the United States was similar. As Macpherson points out, the first wave of Samoan migrants in New Zealand (those who arrived prior to World War II [WWII]) consisted of Samoan scholarship students to theological schools and universities. Similarly, according to Sereisa Milford, migrants from Samoa first came to the United States as members of the Mormon Church to help build the Mormon Temple in Hawai'i in the early 1920s (1985–86, 54). The second wave of migration to both New Zealand and the United States took place after WWII. Samoans who arrived in this wave either had served in colonial bureaucracies (in both independent and American Samoa), had joined the U.S. military during the war, or were *afakasi* (literally half-caste, used to describe people from Samoa of mixed parentage). Most of the migrants to the United States had been involved with the U.S. military base in American Samoa during WWII. The majority of these migrants had lived in Pago Pago, capital of American Samoa. The third wave of migration occurred in the early 1960s when people began to take advantage of the postwar demand for manual labor. By this time, migrants were beginning to think of traveling to New Zealand or the United States as part of larger circuits of travel (Liliomaiava-Doktor 2009a, 2009b). Craig Janes writes that by the early 1960s in America Samoa, "it was clear that migration was becoming institutionalized as a rite of passage for young Samoans" (Janes 1990, 26).

The third wave of Samoan migrants was the largest—both to New Zealand and to the United States. When these migrants first arrived in Los Angeles and San Francisco, the cities were experiencing a postwar boom. As a result, there were plenty of manual labor jobs available, and Samoan migrants quickly fit into a particular socioeconomic niche: men working in factories or at the docks, and women often working as nurses (see Ablon 1971; Pitt and Macpherson 1974). Many Samoan migrants held two or three jobs in an effort to earn enough money to send back to their families in Samoa and American Samoa. All three waves were comprised largely of young adults, who were recently married or about to be married and starting new households. Households were often large, consisting of several close relatives and their children. This is still the case today.

While the waves of migration helped to shape how Samoan communities originally formed in both New Zealand and the United States, these waves have little relevance in people's daily lives now. In fact, it would be a mistake to emphasize them when thinking about Samoan communities today. People travel back and forth between Samoa and other countries regularly (see Lilomaiava-Doktor 2009a, 2009b). They often move back to Samoa for a few years and then return to New Zealand or the United States. Samoan communities in diaspora reflect this greater variability, including people with a wide range of commitments and experiences both in Samoa and in being Samoan. In much the same way that the notion of migrant generations can create erroneous classifications, a rigid scheme of "waves of migration" does not accurately represent the considerable variation within contemporary Samoan communities.

I conducted fieldwork in New Zealand and the United States at a moment when Samoan migrant families were encountering neoliberal changes in government policies toward families (1996–1998). Both New Zealand and U.S. government policies had been shifting toward decentralization and privatization of government services since the early 1980s—beginning with so-called Reaganomics (after President Ronald Reagan) in the United States and Rogernomics (after Finance Minister Roger Douglas) in New Zealand (see Harvey 2005 and Kelsey 1995 for detailed historical overviews). It took time for these policies to begin affecting migrant families. By the mid-1990s, legislation was in place—such as the 1996 Personal Responsibility and Work Opportunity Reconciliation Act in the United States and the 1989 Children, Young Persons, and Their Families Act in New Zealand. These pieces of legislation required families to do much of the labor that governments had earlier taken on as their responsibility (see chapters 4 and 5). My focus is on this historical moment when Samoan families were just beginning to realize that the government systems they had learned to navigate were once again changing fundamentally their terms and structures.

Samoan migrants did not always realize that something like a neoliberal perspective was affecting their encounters with government bureaucracy. They didn't always know that government officials were increasingly emphasizing market rationality (see Gershon 2011). Mostly what they saw was a mysterious and unstable government bureaucracy (in fact, a collection of government bureaucracies) changing yet again. For them, these changes posed new obstacles—and perhaps even offered new possibilities—for what they hoped to accomplish for their families and church communities. As a consequence, Samoan migrants were engaging with neoliberal ideologies in sporadic and incomplete ways. When they experienced the travails of capitalism, as I describe in chapter 1, they still understood it as capitalism writ generic, not a specific version of neoliberal capitalism encouraging them to take their personhood to be metaphorically a business, a collection of assets and skills that must be managed and continually enhanced.

The neoliberal changes that Samoan migrants encountered occurred in two general ways—through changes to the terms by which people classified their daily interactions and through changes to the government infrastructures that Samoan migrants were navigating. Neoliberal perspectives have reconfigured the definitions of terms commonly used to structure bureaucratic ideologies and projects—terms such as responsibility, risk, empowerment, ethnicity, alliances, community, and, most important for my purposes, culture and expertise (see Brown 2006; Comaroff and Comaroff 2009; Coombe 2010; Cruikshank 1999; Maurer 1999; O'Malley 1996). Yet the neoliberal definitions of these terms are reconfigurations, not inventions. As Carol Greenhouse argues: "The 'politics of interpretation' (Cavell 1984, 27 ff.) under neoliberalism is easily missed or evaded by participants and observers alike, given a marked tendency for neoliberal political restructuring and resignification to borrow from older social forms—for example, borrowing the language of rights to sustain markets, citizens' forums to deflect social movements, public office for pursuit of private interests, and credit relationships as channels of social control" (Greenhouse 2010, 4). It is precisely because these terms are given new valences based on older social assumptions that people during my fieldwork were unclear about what the changes were. Government bureaucracies would attempt to devolve responsibility to community-based organizations by arguing for culturally appropriate services. *Culture* in the process became a skill set that certain community workers and social workers possessed as cultural experts that could assist them in dealing with certain clients but not others. Yet Samoan community workers had been arguing for culturally appropriate services for decades before promoting "culturally appropriate" services became a handy explanation for why governments might wish to devolve responsibility to families and communities (see chapter 4). What Samoan migrants understood as culture and what neoliberal government bureaucrats understood as culture only occasionally overlapped, although as my ethnography shows, both sets could find ways to turn the resulting miscommunications to their own advantage.

It wasn't only the terms that were changing as a result of new neoliberal policies; it was also government infrastructures (see Star 1999). Here I draw inspiration from science studies scholars who have turned to studying infrastructures to uncover the ways that taken-for-granted and embedded classificatory systems will enable and limit possibilities for action (Bowker and Star 1999). Neoliberal government policies' emphasis on devolving responsibility to communities involved a substantial shift in the infrastructures that formed the basis for family/government interaction. Bruno Latour and other science studies scholars have turned to the materialities of scientific infrastructure to reveal how scientific "facts" are rendered universal (Latour 1999). In my ethnography, similar uses of infrastructure are used to classify interactions in ways that produce disconnection while simultaneously enabling government bureaucrats to frame their practices as acultural and universal, and to treat their clients as cultural and opaque (on viewing bureaucracy as universal, see also Coles 2007; Tsing 2005).

Neoliberal government policies may have changed the terms and infrastructures that shaped Samoan migrant experiences with governments. But this did not mean that Samoan migrants experienced neoliberalism as a unified project. Instead, the policies entered their lives in halting and sporadic waves, not as clear-cut or well-defined transformations. By focusing on Samoan migrant experiences in 1996 to 1998, I am looking at how a minority migrant group began to respond to neoliberal transformations while simultaneously still engaging with the older forms of government infrastructures that continued to linger. While Samoan migrants were exploring new employment possibilities created by neoliberals' valorization of cultural knowledge as a potential asset on the job market, this view of culture had not yet affected the ways they experienced cultural differences within their families. When my ethnography discusses the traces of neoliberal transformations, it reveals a story of slow encroachments, not radical epistemic shifts.

When Samoans Talk About Culture

In looking at the difference between the cultural and the acultural, I turn to three sites where this was an important issue during my fieldwork: (1) Samoan ritual exchanges *(fa'alavelave)*, (2) conversions between Christian denominations, and (3) interactions between Samoan migrants and government officials. In the first two sites, the dominant question is: How do Samoan migrants understand what is cultural and what is acultural? In the third site, I look at the perspective of both Samoan migrants and government officials. Samoan migrants seemed to be a particularly felicitous group to study when exploring this question because, when asked, they often will talk easily about what constitutes Samoan culture. When I asked a Pacific Island diversity trainer for a New Zealand government agency if Samoan social workers were different from other Pacific Island trainees, he answered by comparing training sessions with people from Samoa and the Cook Islands. In these sessions, he would ask Samoan social workers and Cook Island social workers what their cultural values are. Samoan social workers always answered readily, rattling off four or five values that they thought were core Samoan values.[5] The Cook Islanders always struggled to come up with unifying values. This is not to say that Samoans are much better at being cultural than Cook Islanders. Rather, Samoans were more comfortable describing themselves explicitly as cultural beings using a list of four or five core values.

Other ethnographers of Samoa have documented their interlocutors' comfortable willingness to be explicit about Samoan culture and values[6] in nonbureaucratic contexts (Drozdow-St. Christian 2002; Mageo 1998; Shore 1982; Va'a 2001). As Bradd Shore has pointed out, there are several differently nuanced words in Samoan for culture: *aganu'u, aga,* or *fa'asamoa* (1982, 221–222). Even linguistically, the culture concept and its equivalents are relatively accessible categories for Samoan speakers. Government bureaucrats did not have to teach Samoan migrants that they were culture-bearers; they already knew that they had a culture. The criticism that scholars have levied against bureaucratic treatment of culture—that it presupposes culture is static and rule-governed—has not been a problem that my interlocutors ever voiced. They seemed comfortable joining government bureaucrats in essentializing Samoan culture.

---

5. See Mulitalo-Lauta (2000) for an extended example of common accounts of Samoan culture.

6. This appears to be a historical proclivity on the part of Samoans, providing a counterexample to Roy Wagner's (1981) suggestion that anthropologists might be partially responsible for convincing others that they have a culture.

While both migrants from Samoa and government officials may willingly agree that Samoan culture exists and has an easily defined set of values, this does not mean that culture is invoked in the same way in government contexts and within Samoan families and communities. For example, government officials will tend to interpret differences as cultural after a failure in communication or compliance on the part of the clients. In these instances, often government officials will see themselves as acultural, with the clients as the culture bearers. Government bureaucracies also reify culture, using culture as a formal category for classifying people. Among families, culture is a far more fluid concept, used not only as an explanation for failure but to imagine why people act the ways that they do, to realign what it means to be responsible for particular actions, and to understand why relationships are unfolding in the ways that they are (that is, not necessarily as explanations for failure but more broadly as explanations of process). Government bureaucracies are requiring an essentialized Samoanness that often can obscure a principal project of Samoan migrant families. Samoan families are constantly working to define certain contexts as Samoan, and Samoan migrants often must figure out how to position themselves successfully in Samoan hierarchies while in fundamentally hybrid situations. What is a continual process from the perspective of Samoan families (trying to define contexts and people as cultural) is presumed to be an already given for government bureaucracies. Government bureaucrats already know culture is out there and can be easily identified. In other words, what is relevant in these government contexts is the Samoanness itself as a marker, not, as it is for families, the varied and complicated processes by which contexts and people come to be defined as Samoan. This tension presents quandaries to Samoan migrants when they attempt to navigate government bureaucracies using a variety of strategies discussed in part II.

It is not only government definitions of the cultural and the acultural that creates dilemmas for Samoan migrants. The project of being Samoan itself can produce conundrums, especially as people engage simultaneously with global movements of people, resources, and ideas. For example, in chapter 1, I address the challenges that arise when people try to participate simultaneously in capitalist and Samoan ritual exchanges—two forms of exchange that my interlocutors in the field often felt were antithetical to each other. They found it difficult to be simultaneously a good capitalist and a good Samoan. In chapter 2, I trace how moving between the cultural and the acultural continues to create dilemmas for Samoans as they move between Samoan churches and putatively acultural evangelical Christian churches. Yet the cultural/acultural divide within Samoan communities is experienced and practiced within Samoan communities differently from how it is practiced when Samoans are expected to be culture bearers in government contexts. There is a disconnection between the dynamics in the first part of the book and the second part.

In talking about Samoans, I risk the possibility that some readers will think I am essentializing. I do not mean to say that all people from Samoa think or act or talk in a particular way. I am tracing the shared assumptions that my interlocutors told me through various stories and practices that they used to evaluate others as Samoan, or felt evaluated by themselves. Samoanness is a mutually constituted category that my interlocutors would use to understand certain social unities or moralities, in addition to using the category to predict others' behavior. Samoanness glossed a shared intentional field (Wagner 1981), in which my interlocutors expressed general agreement about what counted as spontaneous or reactive behavior in contexts they framed as Samoan. To be Samoan means to share with others certain epistemological assumptions about what it means to be intentional and to have cultural knowledge. That is, being Samoan involves analyzing why others behave the way that they do from a Samoan perspective. These understandings, like all other such understandings, presuppose that social interactions will unfold in certain ways and require people to improvise creative responses when the social interactions do not unfold as anticipated. In the first half of the book, I discuss the dilemmas that definitions of Samoan culture and its acultural counterpoint (be it the church or capitalism) pose for Samoan families. Rather than essentializing, I am viewing my interlocutors as social analysts who actively use the culture concept in their own right and exploring how they use Samoanness and Samoan culture as analytical categories.

At the same time, I am trying throughout the book to avoid passing judgment on who is Samoan or speaking for Samoan culture. Determining Samoanness was not my task. This is a task that I want to reserve for Samoans, as scholars from Pacific islands have rightly and repeatedly encouraged scholars to do (Hereniko 2000; Teaiwa 2005a and 2005b). I decided that this was not my job prior to even venturing into fieldwork, and I tried to find the moments when Samoan migrants were acting in the interstices of social orders such as Samoan culture and government bureaucracy. I sought out moments where no one is an expert about what truly counts as cultural knowledge. This did not always work, and throughout the book, I am often describing how Samoan migrants represent their cultural expertise in these hybrid moments. My aim is to treat Samoan epistemological assumptions about who gets to speak for and about Samoan culture respectfully. I describe how these epistemological assumptions are not always shared by others, and point out the consequences when they are not. In general, I am interested in figuring out when cultural differences were at stake in the social interactions I observed: When did it make sense to talk about certain interactions as encapsulating colliding cultural expectations? I am stressing the multiplicities of difference, while my interlocutors generally stressed the singularity of culture.

Another caveat: Samoa emerges as a nostalgic utopic space in my interlocutors' imagination,[7] the site of authentic and properly enacted cultural knowledge.[8] The Samoa that people describe does not exist. Rather, it serves as a place marker that people can invoke to comment on certain forms of cultural authority. While this will be familiar to many scholars of diaspora (see Axel 2004), in this book, I discuss the form it takes when migrants negotiate what counts as Samoan cultural knowledge. The Samoa discussed here is the imagined counterpoint to life in the United States or New Zealand—a site where people never have to create Samoanness out of hybridity, since Samoanness *there* is presumed by Samoan migrants to be the natural and pure state.[9]

Chapter Overview

I begin by looking at how people are understood by other Samoans to embody cultural or acultural knowledge, especially as migrants navigate

---

7. My word choice reflects this particular nostalgia. Rather than distinguishing between Western Samoa (now independent Samoa) and American Samoa in my general discussion, I refer to Samoa as a unified territory in much the same way that my interlocutors in the field would.

8. Douglass St. Christian (1994) argues that in Samoa people describe the *fa'asamoa* as a similar utopic possibility. "While *Fa'a Samoa* is spoken of as a totalizing code, it is a code which is sought after or pursued, rather than adhered to or obeyed. It is, as one informant put it to me, 'a Samoan's dream of what Samoa should be', a process of desire, rather than a fixed standard of regulation" (33).

9. Both American Samoa and (independent) Samoa are far more multicultural than Samoan migrants tended to describe in conversation.

the two mutually incompatible demands of capitalism and Samoan ritual exchange. This chapter is based on interviews with Samoan families in Auckland, Wellington, and San Francisco, as well as my participation in different church communities for two and a half years. In chapter 1, "Exchanging While Not-Knowing," I focus on the practices of eliciting money and other resources for ritual exchanges as moments in which Samoan migrants do not simultaneously engage with Samoan cultural exchanges or "acultural" capitalist exchanges. I explore the ways Samoan migrants see their own cultural identity as synonymous with participating in fashioning durable exchange relations across distances, and the conundrums this poses for them when surrounded by capitalist exchanges.

Chapter 2, "The Moral Economies of Conversion," examines the ways Christianity is framed at different moments as alternately cultural and acultural when people convert from one form of Christianity to another. Conversion narratives are rich sites for examining how these distinctions are constructed as Samoan migrants describe moving from Samoan Christianities to evangelical and less "cultural" churches. Christianity has had a complex history in Samoa, figured as both a moral modern way to live and as fundamentally Samoan. The evangelical Christian movements have caused Samoan migrants to reframe their relationships to both Christianity and culture. These contemporary conversions require that Samoan migrants attribute meaning and meaninglessness anew to various forms of Christian worship, generating reflexive explanations of their personal transformations as movements between the cultural and the acultural.

In my third site, government–Samoan interactions, I discuss the ways that nation-states have responded to global flows of people and developed policy-driven definitions of what constitutes "culture" and "ethnicity" through long-term dealings with dominant minorities. When government officials then address representatives of minor minority groups, such as Samoan migrants, the officials expect them to respond according to these established expectations. Migrants enter contexts where the challenge is not establishing the terms of the debate but rewriting them.

The third chapter, "When Culture Is Not a System," addresses one of the ways government officials respond to their multicultural migrant clients and colleagues—by requiring cultural brokers. I begin with a dilemma for Samoan cultural brokers: whereas governments rely on and even reward minority representatives who can serve as cultural mediators,

Samoans find such mediators to be contentious figures. Members of Samoan communities often view them as treacherous and reject their assistance. By looking at how and why Samoan migrants reject these brokers, I uncover hitherto unexplored tensions between belonging to a system and belonging to a culture in multicultural policies. This U.S.–based chapter addresses how reflexivity structures the ways that people navigate contexts with multiple social orders. I argue that government officials understand culture from a bureaucratic system's perspective, believing that dealing with multiple cultures requires the same skills as dealing with multiple bureaucracies. In this sense, government agencies view cultural knowledge from a putatively acultural perspective, rewarding people with multiple cultural fluencies. Samoan communities' distrust of cultural brokers, in contrast, emerges from how Samoan migrants understand the relationships one should have to cultural knowledge. From a Samoan perspective, being able to move between cultures indicates that one's connection to one's culture is arbitrary and discardable. Samoan migrants often view mediators as betraying cultural imperatives and as potentially treacherous. These mediators are seen as having the potential to act against their own communities' interests precisely because of their apparent ability to transition between cultures.

Chapter 4 turns to the consequences of neoliberal reforms for the government–family divide. I address how a New Zealand family law legislates what qualifies as a cultural family in ways that contradict how Samoan families circulate knowledge. In passing this legislation, members of Parliament explicitly attempted to respond to the needs of a multicultural nation. The Children, Young Persons, and Their Families Act (1989) transformed how government agencies were supposed to respond to cases of child abuse and juvenile crime in an attempt to fashion a bureaucracy that could be flexible in response to cultural families. Yet because of the ways in which Samoan family hierarchies now stretch across oceans and are not always present in one locale, Samoan families do not circulate knowledge according to the ways the Act presupposes that they will.

In chapter 5, I turn to a common experience for migrants in general: how raising children far from where the parents grew up can focus attention on the consequences of migrating into multiculturalism. I consider ways that migrants evoke terms implicating culture and assimilation to understand how youth become icons for debating how best to navigate cultural and acultural spaces. In both New Zealand and the United States, Samoan communities publicly discussed the problems their youth presented—not being respectful enough, not speaking Samoan well enough, and so on. The youth also described encountering problems that were often the exact inverse of what their parents saw as the problems—they were not accepted by Samoan communities as Samoan enough but faced prejudice for being Samoan in school and at work. Migrants in both countries were interpreting generation gaps as cultural gaps, although with different solutions. In New Zealand, Samoan migrants told me that the children needed to be taught Samoan culture. In the United States, Samoan migrants insisted that the parents needed to be taught another approach, the American way. This difference in framing affects the solutions Samoan migrants advocate when rearing children. In this chapter, I explore in detail how Samoan community workers in the United States attempt to teach Samoan parents to think about Samoan culture in a new way, to see Samoan culture as something that one can choose to enact rather than something one is born enacting.

In turning to the moments when Samoan culture is defined vis-à-vis its opposite, be that capitalism, evangelical Christianity, or government bureaucracy, I build on Arjun Appadurai's call in *Modernity at Large* to examine not culture, but cultural difference: "The most valuable feature of the concept of culture is the concept of difference, a contrastive rather than substantive property of certain things.... [C]ulture is not usefully regarded as a substance but is better regarded as a dimension of phenomena, a dimension that attends to situated and embodied difference. Stressing the dimensionality of culture rather than its substantiality permits our thinking of culture less a property of individuals and groups and more as a heuristic device that we can use to talk about difference" (1996, 12–13). Culture is not only a heuristic device for me to address difference; it is a heuristic device for people in my various fieldsites to produce differences that alternatively act to assist or oppose people's strategies. Throughout the book, I examine how people's reflexive understandings contribute to the ways in which Samoan migrants and government officials make some differences cultural.

In the wake of anthropological critiques of the culture concept, ethnographers have been faced with a dilemma: How does one address cultural differences and the multiple perspectives that exist in so many contemporary contexts without re-creating the problems associated with the culture concept? By turning to how people's own social analysis contributes to epistemological differences, I am providing one ethnographically grounded solution that other anthropologists also have found useful long before me. Reflexivity is central to how Samoan migrants drew the lines between putatively acultural capitalist exchanges and ritual exchanges, between government views of culture and their own. To understand how differences are made cultural, one can turn to people's own social analysis of the social orders around them, beginning with people's reflexive understandings of their social worlds.

Part I

1

EXCHANGING WHILE NOT-KNOWING

Samoan migrants are constantly finding themselves in situations where multiple social orders are at play. This may be most obvious when they enter government offices or in courts of law, where they face institutionalized systems that operate by principles that are often antithetical to Samoan strategies. However, Samoan migrants also have to navigate multiple social orders in some moments that might seem most Samoan, such as Samoan ritual exchanges. To hold a Samoan wedding, funeral, or to bestow a *matai* (chiefly) title, many people have to move resources (cash and commodities) from capitalist exchanges into Samoan ritual exchanges (*fa'alavelave*[1]). Capitalist exchanges don't operate by the same principles as Samoan ritual exchanges, so that Samoans are constantly moving among two distinct and, on the surface, incompatible exchange systems. How do people manage to participate in two ways of ordering social interactions that

---

1. Shore defines *fa'alavelave* as cultural entanglements. Samoans used the term primarily to describe exchange rituals (Shore 1982, 243).

clash? In part I of this book, I explore how people do so within Samoan communities, in contexts that all participants agree are Samoan contexts—*fa'alavelave* and churches. I look at how knowledge circulation plays a central role, including in this chapter especially moments when knowledge doesn't circulate. I explore how people's practices and social analysis can help ensure that they aren't engaging with two incompatible social orders simultaneously, but rather are moving *between* the two. I also look at how framing certain practices as cultural and others as acultural helps people to navigate opposing or mutually exclusive social orders.[2]

Why turn first to *fa'alavelave*, to Samoan ritual exchanges? In Samoan migrant contexts, talking about culture invariably involves talking about ritual exchanges. In my conversations, *fa'asamoa* (the Samoan way) often referred to Samoan culture as a whole, or specifically to *fa'alavelave* (Samoan ritual exchanges; often weddings, funerals, title bestowal ceremonies, or birthdays). The ease underpinning this semantic slippage from *fa'asamoa* to *fa'alavelave* is no accident. For many that I spoke with, being a cultural person means participating in some form in Samoan ritual exchanges. By contrast, capitalist exchange is widely understood to be acultural. People are constantly involved in both forms of exchange relationships, they were frequently moving between exchanges they considered cultural and exchanges they considered acultural. But this movement is not seamless.

I was reminded of how difficult it was to move between both exchange systems when I was chatting with one of my Samoan friends in Auckland about a recent funeral in her family. I asked her how much her parents expected her to contribute. They wanted two hundred dollars, which surprised me. I knew that she and her son lived with her parents and paid the highest rent of all her siblings—$260 NZ a fortnight. She was a single mother, technically unemployed because she was a student, so all her money came from government benefits. She also regularly paid the phone bill, which was often $400 NZ a month. I mentally added it up: $920 NZ for that month. "Don't they know how little you get?" I asked in confusion. She shrugged—"They don't act like it." Yet, at the same time, I knew how important participating in *fa'alavelave* was for my friend, and many other Samoans. These were moments in which people's family connections

---

2. Goddard (2000) calls for such a focus on the praxis of exchange in distinguishing between capitalist and gift exchanges.

and love were publicly performed and made tangible. To say no would be to deny one of the most central ways of being Samoan.

This conversation was reminiscent of many interviews and conversations I had with other Samoan migrants and their in-laws about how much was constantly expected of them by family relatives. In an interview, a European New Zealand woman married to a Samoan man raised in New Zealand told me that she was at her wits end because her father-in-law, who lived in Auckland, was demanding $5,000 for his local church. She and her husband simply did not have the money, yet saying no was not an option. She was worried that they would have to take out a bank loan, and then another and another every time a *fa'alavelave* came up. She kept wondering when these demands would end, and I felt empathetically dismayed as we both agreed that there was no end in sight. And yet how could her husband deny his father and his father's pride in his family? Hearing my friend telling me about her latest financial pressures from her parents, I began to realize what people had been telling me all along—that when migrants made requests from a Samoan perspective, they did not take into account how limited other people's resources were. For those being asked, it feels as though their elders' initial assumption is that other people are potentially boundless resources and this potential wealth can be tapped into through carefully established strategies.

Those asking for resources were consistently overlooking other people's position in a capitalist system, and, in doing so, refusing to manage the intricacies of capitalism and *fa'alavelave* at the same time. It was the job of those receiving the appeal to establish the limits of their resources as strategically and inoffensively as they could, to figure out how to move their resources into Samoan exchanges.

When I heard that, in her parents' eyes, my friend had sufficient, albeit unknown, resources for long costly phone calls, high rent, and funeral donations, another tendency solidified for me that I had been noticing half-consciously. Like some readers' experiences in other contexts, no one in the Samoan families I met knew exactly how much money and resources other family members had. Family members had quite good guesses about what others might be earning at a job, but these were just guesses.[3] Family

---

3. This not-knowing was even institutionalized in the ways that Samoan migrants responded to government forms administered by nonprofit organizations in both New Zealand and

members went to great lengths not to reveal exactly how much they had, a strategy designed to enable them to exert some control over where their resources would go. This was a not-knowing that Samoans quite consciously maintained, both those asking for resources and those being asked, elicitors and elicitees alike. It was a central strategy for being part of two incompatible exchange systems, and also one that was seen as a strategy more commonly used after migration.

People often told me that Samoans cannot openly withhold any of their widely known resources without giving serious offense. My interlocutors during fieldwork insisted that in Samoa, there were multiple indirect ways to say no—such as letting the air out of the tires and claiming the truck was broken instead of loaning the truck. Outside of Samoa, migrants believed that similar tactics were less successful. Those I interviewed were often nostalgic for a Samoa where similar "accidents" could supply external refusals to voiced demands. Yet they also claimed that certain strategic forms of ignorance are far more common and effective after migration than while in Samoa.

People claimed that outside of Samoan villages, it is much more common to create the space to refuse aid by not letting others know how much one actually has. If this ambiguity has been achieved, the family members can protest that they simply do not have the resources when their family collects for Samoan functions. This is not, however, always a successful strategy and often has unwelcome consequences. If someone repeatedly refuses to contribute, they risk being excluded from these family functions. With this potential retribution in mind, family members would try to create some room in which they could maneuver by not letting anyone else know what resources were at their disposal.

At the same time, they are often and easily complaining about how other people respond to this uncertainty. I have heard many Samoans (and often their non-Samoan spouses) say, "people back home in Samoa [or "my family here"] don't realize I have lots of expenses here. They don't realize I have to pay the rent and the phone bill and the electricity bill." These anxieties were provoked by elicitors who lived in the same house,

---

California. Especially in the United States, the Samoan community workers would never expect an accurate number when filling out the question "household income." Instead, they expected only an approximation of the applicant's own income.

down the street, in the same neighborhood, or in Samoa. For other migrant groups, distance is a determining factor in establishing how wealthy others are perceived to be. Relatives in other countries are often imagined to be wealthier than relatives living next door. This is not the case for Samoans. The relationship I focus on here–between elicitor and elicitee–is *not* confined to elicitors living in Samoa and elicitees living overseas. Participants can be as far apart as New Zealand and Massachusetts, or both can live in the same household. While distance creates opportunities for strategic ignorance that do not require daily maintenance, the difference is one of degree, not substantive practice. Spatial proximity made little difference to elicitors' demands and elicitees' limited ability to mitigate the amount. After all, this strategy of not-knowing was attempting to solve the dilemma of operating within two incompatible exchange systems, a dilemma that nowadays exists everywhere for Samoans.

These moments are endemic to modern experiences of being Samoan, both in diaspora and in the Samoan islands. To be Samoan, people everywhere are using money they earn to participate in translocal Samoan exchanges and thus bettering their family's social status within Samoan communities that can be local or elsewhere in the Samoan Pacific. My interlocutors are not experiencing their exchange system as *pre-capitalist,* but rather as a contemporaneous alternative to capitalism and culturally specific. The experiences I am addressing in this chapter are ones that, despite my expectations and my interlocutors' perceptions, are not dependent on location. In practice they engage in a hybrid of Samoan and capitalist exchanges constantly regardless of whether they live in Apia or Auckland. And while some contexts are defined by all participants as Samoan or capitalist, the actual practices are never as homogeneously one or the other, despite how participants openly define the context.

When families demand money from migrant members for Samoan obligations, the elicitors often ignore the capitalist context, the labor, and restrictions in which people acquire their resources, no matter how near or far away these family members are. Those who elicit rely on the strategic room generated by not knowing others' resources fully, as much as those who were supposed to provide the resources. Thus, this not-knowing acts as a double-edged sword, creating a strategic space that allow misapprehensions that potentially benefit the elicitors as well as the elicited. Intriguingly, those who elicit are often being asked to contribute themselves by people higher in their family's hierarchy, and often for the same ritual exchange. Yet they often will not interpret others' pressures in light of their own. They are reluctant to project the resource limitations that restrict what they can give onto those from whom they themselves elicit resources. Samoan migrants are refusing to engage *simultaneously* in two incompatible systems as they are shifting resources from an arena dominated by the supposedly acultural capitalism[4] to an arena determined by Samoan exchange system, which was understood by my interlocutors to be cultural.

I am arguing that Samoans, in order to continue the hybrid collage of exchanges they practice daily, are actively re-creating and distinguishing between two perspectives on exchange–capitalist (and putatively acultural) and Samoan exchange (understood as cultural). They do not use objects to demarcate these two perspectives.[5] There are two vending machines in the San Francisco church hall where I watched many Samoan ritual exchanges, and participants will use soda cans from these machines in place of coconuts when presenting money and cloth to the other parties in the exchange. This is a small and not so charged moment of apparent crossover, "modern" objects could be easily used in rituals without much comment. Instead of using objects to demarcate when an exchange was not capitalist, they use certain patterns of knowledge transmission to distinguish between these two perspectives.

Most scholars writing about movements between two different exchange systems have focused on the tensions surrounding the units of exchange, such as from shells to coins, as they circulate (Akin and Robbins 1999; Bohannon 1959; Graeber 1996; Keane 2001; Parry and Bloch 1989). Since Paul Bohannon's seminal article (1959), anthropologists have focused on how objects move between spheres of exchange, emphasizing the interaction between distinct systems of interwoven social relationships, exchange guidelines, and objects. In much of the literature, spheres of exchange are always already differentiated. The dilemma, for both those exchanging and the analysts, is to uncover the principles that will allow objects to move between these spheres. The underlying ethnographic questions have centered around how new exchange systems

4. From my ethnographic perspective, the capitalism that Samoans practiced was a Samoan-inflected capitalism. Yet the people involved perceived capitalism as an acultural form of exchange.
5. This is historically true as well; see Linnekin 1991: 2–3.

or objects will reconfigure social relationships. In short, anthropologists' focus on objects has gone hand in hand with a concern about the extent to which translation between spheres is also a transformation of value systems.

By focusing on the flow of objects as the starting point for unpacking exchange, anthropologists have also attributed a certain generativity to the objects. As Sharon Hutchinson points out about Bohannon's framework, "it is premised on the idea that 'things-in-themselves,' rather than the so-cial relations through which they flow, differentiate 'spheres of exchange'" (Hutchinson 1996, n. 90). Hutchinson proceeds in *Nuer Dilemmas* to de-scribe how the Nuer distinguish types of money so as to differentiate mar-ket and kinship social relations (Hutchinson 1996, 83–102). For the Nuer, money in itself is not sufficient to differentiate between social relations. Money that came from work, for example, was different from money that came from the sale of cattle. The Nuer will use hybrid categories that refer to both cattle and monetary exchange, such as "the money of cattle" for money acquired through the sale of cattle, or "the cattle of money" for purchased cattle (Hutchinson 1996: 56). These categories are entangl-ing precisely those spheres of exchange that Bohannon might expect to be kept differentiated. In Hutchinson's analysis, spheres of exchange become indigenous categories that do not possess the clear-cut boundaries that previous ethnographic studies were presuming. Following Hutchinson's lead, I am asking here not about how the circulating objects might create different exchange spheres but rather about how people circulate knowl-edge about exchange and resources to produce boundaries between two systems that can thus become distinct.

Contrary to what a "spheres of exchange" approach would predict, Sa-moan migrants must labor to produce an arena of exchange that is de-marcated as Samoan, and thus cultural. "Acultural" capitalist and Samoan exchanges are in practice intermeshed for Samoans; money and com-modities (including, but not limited to, bright manufactured cloth, *leis* of Tootsie Rolls, and kegs of corned beef) flow through Samoan hands easily and in all directions. I have found that people do not primarily rely on ob-jects to differentiate between capitalist exchanges and Samoan exchanges. They are not terribly concerned about purifying or recontextualizing the markers of supposedly acultural capitalisms in order to make these objects Samoan. Capitalism and commodity fetishism in themselves are not what people are rejecting when trying to form a Samoan space alongside capitalist arenas.

Experiencing "Acultural" Capitalism

As I was reading over my field notes in preparation to write about Samoan exchange, I kept searching for Samoan critiques of capitalism; for example, accounts of how poorly paid workers are or grumblings about bosses. These were strikingly absent. Instead, I had jotted down many instances in which my interviewees idealized a putatively acultural capitalism in two ways—either by criticizing other Samoans for being bad capitalists or, more commonly, bemoaning their own inability to accumulate. I heard a typical critique of other Samoans' economic decisions when a woman in her late twenties told me about how her aunt had for years chosen to work at an hourly rate even though her employers kept offering to give her a permanent position with benefits. Her aunt refused, preferring the opportunity to earn overtime. Her niece told me this as an example of how Samoans do not plan ahead, how they live only for the short term. This type of critique was common in my fieldwork conversations as people would tell me how other Samoans, as a general category, refused to strategize for the long term in capitalist contexts. This was often accompanied by a discussion of their own inability to save or even control their money. Any money they had would be used for unexpected extended family demands: to assist with a funeral or be sent back with an unplanned visitor from Samoa. One Samoan-raised woman I interviewed told me: "When I first came over, it was to have a job.... It was to have a job and to help the family in Samoa. You know, once I had the job, when they [her family] knew, they keep writing that so-and-so [needs money] and then I give up. I said to myself, 'probably I did the wrong thing.' You know, like every month I send a hundred dollars. If I add all that up, probably I can buy a house by now."

In both these moments of idealizing capitalism, people I spoke with are longing for the same thing: for money to be more than just a commodity. They were telling me that the intersection between Samoan and "acultural" capitalist exchanges limits the ways in which people can employ money. For my interlocutors, money functions as cash—a commodity with immediate use potential. This is culturally specific. In other ethnographic accounts, people not only recognized that money can produce more money but also described this property as magical. Michael Taussig (1980) describes how Bolivian miners realize this capitalist mystification in the following passage:

> Therefore, the task facing the inhabitants of the plantation zones in the southern Cauca Valley is how to explain, and in some cases actually effect, the transformation of properties of similarity into those of difference and those of difference into those of similarity. They must explain how characteristics that were once the exclusive property of animals are now ascribed to money, the natural property of which is to remain barren. They must explain the transformation of money into interest-bearing capital and the conversion of use-value into exchange value. (131)

In Taussig's account, Bolivian peasants explore how, to operate in a capitalist system, one must actively misrecognize certain relationships among labor, money, and commodities, by, for instance, treating money as able to multiply like animals do. These peasants are being bad capitalists because they are finding these misrecognitions unsettling, and are unwilling to adopt them readily.

In a sense, people are being bad *Samoan* capitalists because they are applying an unproductive misrecognition when they manage their money. Instead of treating money as a form of marking value whose links to commodities can be manipulated to produce more money, people treat money as though it was yet another commodity. When my interlocutors complained that they wanted to save money, they were also saying that dwelling in this intersection prevented them from using money as potential, a convertible resource that can multiply on its own. Their family's demands compel them to treat money through the lens of commodity fetishism, instead of the lens of interest-bearing capital.

It is not that people are unaware of different forms of exchange when they are operating in a given arena. To exchange, they must act as if they are misrecognizing certain aspects about their own labor, regardless of what they actually think (Žižek 1989, 31). To not know in the moment of practice enables people to transverse capitalist and Samoan exchange systems as though they are shifting perspectives, not enmeshing exchange systems.

Samoan Exchanges

In American Samoa and independent Samoa, *fa'alavelave* serve as a public arena for exploring the boundaries between families, defining family
membership, and revealing the collective strength of a family through its
exchanges. In diaspora, the emphasis on *fa'alavelave* has gradually centered
on exhibiting the strength of the family by revealing the money and fine
mats the family can gather for an event. After migration, being part of a Samoan collectivity has become largely defined in terms of these exchanges.

In the Samoan islands, there is a continuum through which extended
families could articulate forms of relatedness, and thus different degrees
of unity and conflict. *Fa'alavelave* might be the most public forums, but
they are not the primary ones. As the most public arena, these rituals are
sites for families to foreground their unity. During the actual exchange, the
family presents itself as a unified collective, relegating to the background
all the negotiations that go into collecting the exchanged money, food, and
fine mats. During an exchange, what is concealed are the many acts of
eliciting within the families; what is revealed is both the family's wealth
and the family's assessment of its relationship to other families, both competitive and obligatory. Intrafamily networks of exchanges are concealed
in order to reveal interfamily connections. This carries over in diaspora:
migrants experience what it means to be part of a Samoan extended family
largely in terms of the tension between the delicate private elicitations and
the public displays of unity.

What are some of the principles central to making exchanges Samoan;
that is, the public Samoanness that behind-the-scenes elicitations help
make visible? Matori Yamamoto has pointed out that while there is a certain amount of local variation in Samoan migrant exchange practices, there
are also overarching structural commonalities from Apia to Anchorage
(Yamamoto 1997). Yamamoto describes these commonalities as a typology
of specific rituals: title bestowals, weddings, and funerals. Bradd Shore, by
contrast, discusses how Samoan exchanges have different ways of creating equivalences between families and objects exchanged. Shore delineates
two general categories into which Samoan competitive exchanges[6] tend to

---

6. I am restricting my summary of Samoan exchange to the rituals in which exchanges constitute families as units. My account omits a form of exchange that Bradd Shore calls *asymmetrical,*
in which "the focus is on balanced reciprocity and the stabilization of relations between exchange

fall: indirect and direct. In indirect exchanges, each party contributes to the same person or institution. For example, every family contributes money to the church. In Samoan churches following in the London Missionary Society's tradition, at the end of every service, the names of the people and the amounts they contributed are read out loud by a church deacon. The competition is in the indirect exchange; church members want to be seen as donating generously. I noticed that sometimes, if other rival families have donated more that week, a child will be hurriedly sent up to the deacon with an envelope filled with more money. In these instances, those exchanging can quickly compare, and remedy, what they donate in relation to others' donations. Giving is unidirectional; those receiving are under no obligation to reciprocate. Partially as result of this unidirectionality, the exchanges are not attempts to fashion equivalencies between unlike objects. Rather, people are using apparent equivalencies—like families donating like objects—to determine each family's social status.

While indirect exchange assumes a form of equivalence and allows people to generate social differentiation, Shore describes direct, or complementary, competitive exchange as almost an inversion. Complementary, direct exchange creates equivalences between fundamentally unlike objects. For Samoan family events such as weddings, funerals, or title bestowals, the involved families will divide into two groups and exchange the objects appropriate to each side. In the case of a wedding, the bride's side will gather together fine mats, which they will offer the groom's side. In return, the families related to the groom will gather together food, cloth, and canoes, which they will offer in turn. By the 1950s, the groom's side also began to offer cash (Schoeffel, personal communication, 1997). The bride's side also has begun to offer cash during the wedding. Shore argues that the distinction between the objects is based on use value. Fine mats only have *exchange value,* they are stored carefully in sisters or mothers' trunks until they are required for a special occasion. The groom's side offers objects with *use value,* such as kegs of corned beef or bolts of cloth. In the process of ensuring that the groom's side provided enough food and money to be commensurate with the bride's side's offering of fine mats, those exchanging created an equivalency that did not necessarily exist previously. Now that both sides use money in the exchanges, the fact that these exchanges

---

partners through the reinforcement of differentiation" (Shore 1982, 205). These exchanges do not generate a different form of elicitation within families, and so I am omitting a detailed description.

will produce equivalencies has become that much more explicit. People have a general sense of each fine mat's monetary value (in 1998 a bundle of ten not-so-good fine mats was worth approximately one hundred dollars—both in U.S. and New Zealand dollars). As a result, these exchanges also enable families to differentiate themselves socially, and more directly, with the other families with whom they are exchanging.

In preparing for complementary exchanges, according to my observations, a moment when each side does not exchange directly with the other side, the production of equivalencies can be more circuitous. A branch of the bride's family might have gathered together two thousand dollars for a wedding. This will be the accumulated contributions of four local siblings and their adult children. The *matai,* or chief, of that branch will bring the money to the bride's parents, who will refuse to take the entire two thousand dollars. The bride's parents will insist on returning a certain amount of the money, and the amount returned will be the subject of heated debate (the bride's parents typically wanting to return more, and their relatives insisting on giving as much as possible to the wedding). The bride's parents then will distribute the money in various necessary avenues. Some of the money might go to the number of ministers who attend the wedding, some to the various wedding expenses (such as the caterer), and some to the various *tulafale* (talking chiefs) who attend.

In addition, the comparison between what the bride's side contributed in contrast with the groom's side is often not apparent in the moments of exchange, but rather is determined afterward as those present recount the origins and circulatory path of the food, money, and fine mats. The bride's side also will keep a book, in which they record who has contributed various amounts and items, creating equivalences through this inscription. Few people have access to these books. While the heads of the families who contributed will be acknowledged publicly, the exact nature of these contributions is recorded privately. What is publicly apparent are the resources, the power of each family to uphold its honor and gather enough money, food, and fine mats.

These public exchanges forge family unities and differentiations at the same time. In the moment of exchange, the families present themselves as unified collectives that can accumulate a certain amount of money and food. The Samoan families disguise the discord that can go into any pooling of resources from people with many demands on their resources, instead highlighting the successful accumulation. At the same time that the various branches of a family use these ritual spaces to reveal themselves as a harmonious and giving unit, they are also differentiating themselves.

This differentiation occurs in two ways. First, and particularly in the context of migration, these ritual exchanges are the times at which branches of a family determine when they are too distant to be donating to another family's event. By not contributing, or offering only a token amount, that branch begins the process of disentangling from certain relatives. In some cases, families would bring food or money to a funeral, and be turned away because they were not closely related enough to warrant participating in the exchange. This does not seem to happen often after migrating; I only heard about this as a possibility that is not practiced anymore. Second, by exchanging between the two sides, people are also differentiating between families; after all, this is evidence that the families are distinct enough that they can exchange. Exchanging in the Samoan system is always also a marker of separation, delineating the boundaries between families. Sometimes, a branch of a family will be related to both sides, which forces the head of the family to choose judiciously which exchange relationships they want to maintain in that event. I did come across various instances while I interviewed people in which the head of the family had decided to contribute twice to the same event, so as to sustain both exchange relations. These private negotiations are often concealed by the public assertions of separateness that are performed through the exchange.

The publicly performed exchanges are accompanied, especially upon migration, by a complex series of private elicitations that make the actual exchanges that much more of a hidden and satisfying accomplishment. The heads of families never know until the final moments exactly how much money and how many fine mats they will be able to contribute. Occasionally they have to compensate with more of their own resources to ensure that the amount given matches the one they believe the family should contribute. This tension can make these ritual exchanges quite exciting for those organizing the contributions. In fact, because people may learn about weddings or funerals with little advance warning, the energy of pulling it off at the last minute courses through the preparations and elicitations. The calm public displays of family wealth conceal the dramas of near failures and barely overcome last-minute hitches. Graceful public exchanges are counterpoints to the tense private preparations.

The Morality of Eliciting

These elicitations are not only the hectic and energizing build-up to *fa'alavelave;* they are also the sites where people begin demarcating the two exchange perspectives as distinct. While I was interviewing members of Samoan families in both New Zealand and California, I collected many stories about how family members elicit resources from each other. The majority of these stories were told by people receiving the requests—people between the ages of eighteen and forty-five whose parents or local older relatives regularly asked for assistance with family obligations. I did talk to older family members who described their strategies for eliciting and deciding how much to elicit, but for the most part, this next section emerges from interviewees from whom money was collected.

Eliciting takes place in two stages in a Samoan family. In the first instance, the heads of the family must be informed about the looming *fa'alavelave.* This happens through church announcements at the end of the service, by accidental word of mouth (a family member happens to run into a bearer of news), or through systematic phone calls. I interviewed a number of people who admitted that they dreaded answering the phone at six in the morning (and sometimes did not), because they knew that it was bound to be a family member from Samoa asking for help with a funeral or church activity. In my interviews, I was constantly impressed by how effective apparently haphazard communication turned out to be. At this level of interaction, people can find out by chance when an event is happening (although church services were crucial exceptions to this).

Once the heads of families know about an event, there is nothing haphazard about how they contact the rest of the family. They will either call everyone up (having decided in advance how much money should be given) and ask for contributions or call a family meeting. Penny Schoeffel (1999) describes the format of these meetings:

> At this initial meeting, approximate targets of money and goods, usually including fine mats, are decided upon, and agreement is reached as to how much each constituent sub-family group or household (for example, the parents, siblings, first cousins, their adult married children) will respectively contribute and a date is set to pool the fine mats (if required) and money.... Each sub-family then raises their assigned quota, usually drawing

on donations from their affines, and on the appointed date meet in convoca-
tion to announce, display and pool their contributions. In overseas communities the garage is usually decorated with mats to serve as an impromptu
meeting house. It is common for sub-families to vie with one another to ex-
ceed the targets assigned to them. (137)

Often the subfamily holds regular family meetings every week or every
month in which the amount each member will contribute is decided.[7] In
some families, each adult family member contributes a certain amount
every week to a common *fa'alavelave* account. The family meeting will
then involve deciding how much of that pot of money will be used for the
fa'alavelave. In some cases, each family member is expected to contribute
$100 or $200 for the event. Occasionally, the head of the family will stag-
ger the amount, determining whose circumstances might allow a family
member to provide more money. In general, Samoan family heads will
request, and it will be up to the subordinate family members to find the
necessary amount.

What I have just described seems like relatively straightforward methods for collecting money in families with clear-cut hierarchical roles. Yet,
as I mentioned earlier, people were frequently telling me how frustrated
and trapped they felt, how *fa'alavelave* had gotten out of control since
migration (a comment that could segue into a discussion about how, in
Samoa, the *fa'alavelave* were much more manageable). The people I was
interviewing were trapped not by structural contradictions inherent to
Samoan exchanges. Rather, they were caught because they were moving
between two incompatible systems. Living only within the Samoan system seemed to people to be much more manageable than having to be a
capitalist too.

Fa'alavelave's Janus Face

Because *fa'alavelave* are financially draining, my interlocutors have mixed
feelings about participating in them. A typical conversation I had with

---

7. In this instance I am referring to older parents and a sibling group composed of married
and unmarried siblings and their children.

two Samoan women during a church lunch addressed common ambiva-lences. I was watching a young girl deliver an envelope filled with money to a visiting preacher, her T-shirt declaring: "I love my *aiga* (family), but I hate *fa'alavelave.*" I pointed this out to the women sitting next to me, amused by this apparent caption to the ritual. The women nodded in agreement with the slogan. One woman relayed that she found this partic-ular church's *fa'alavelave* especially burdensome; her family was constantly donating money to the church that they sorely needed for household ex-penses. She explained how difficult it was to obey the *fa'asamoa* of this church, using *fa'asamoa* in this context to refer not just to Samoan cul-ture but more specifically to the ritual exchanges. She had grown up in the Mormon Church[8] and had encountered such constant *fa'alavelave* only when, because of marriage, she joined the Congregational Church. By that point in my fieldwork, I had heard many people express similar reserva-tions about *fa'alavelave.* I also knew the flip side to this anxiety, the pride in being part of one's family and part of a Samoan community, and, in-deed, after I asked a few judiciously placed questions, the same woman told me how much she valued all that she had learned about her culture by attending this church. She said that she didn't know her *fa'asamoa* (in this case, culture) before she started attending. The cultural knowledge she was lauding came precisely by observing the Samoan exchanges that also proved burdensome. This conversation, with its apparent contradic-tions, was in many ways an exegesis of the T-shirt slogan, revealing how Samoan migrants feel trapped between obligation and cultural insight as they use their resources publicly to express commitment to their families and their culture.

To say "I love my family, but I hate the ritual exchanges I must do to demonstrate that love" epitomizes the paradox in which Samoan mi-grants find themselves. It articulates a distinction—between family and *fa'alavelave*—that is utterable only from the perspective of the elicitee. The elicitee differentiates among household, family, and *fa'alavelave,* seeing separable units where the elicitor sees manifestations of a unity. Here is

---

8. As I discuss in chapter 2, one of the incentives for people involved in Samoan exchange to join the Mormon Church, along with spiritual reasons, is that membership is less of a financial burden than churches historically linked to the London Missionary Society, which incorporate *fa'alavelave* in their weekly activities.

another moment in which the cultural and acultural are fashioned into distinct perspectives. The elicitor believes that all households are committed toward supporting the family's contributions in any appropriate ritual. Elicitees experience these demands as one set among many—none of which can ever be satisfactorily met without serious consequences in the other neglected arenas. The T-shirt slogan distinguished between family and exchange, but this rarely happened in my interviews. When I talked to Samoan migrants about *fa'alavelave*, elicitees discussed their unease in terms of being torn between using limited resources for their household and supporting their extended family. One schoolteacher who I chatted with over lunch described how she felt this tension. She said that she was just now beginning to evaluate her attitude toward *fa'alavelave;* that she was no longer as willing to give automatically whenever her father called with a request. She said that the moment came when her son asked her for new sneakers. She started explaining to him that they didn't have the money to spend on new shoes, and then stopped. Her father had asked her two days earlier for money for a relative's funeral (whom she did not know), and she had given unquestioningly. At that moment, she realized that she gave money for *fa'alavelave* without reservation, but always tried to cut corners in her own household. She saw her household's needs as flexible enough to be deferred and as less of a priority than her *aiga*'s needs. I heard versions of this story many times, in which a person was forced to juggle the demands of maintaining a home with the demands of being part of a larger Samoan family. While this tension is not unique to migrants, the reasons my interlocutors find the situation to be a catch-22 and the strategies they use in response are bound up with the epistemological assumptions underlying what it means to be part of a Samoan family and also a capitalist exchange system.

In migration, *fa'alavelave* are often the only means through which Samoan families explore their interconnectedness.[9] In American Samoa and independent Samoa, there are many opportunities to express allegiance to an extended family; not so in diaspora. Siblings who haven't seen each other for twenty years might have to interact because of the expenses of a wedding. Peoples' primary connection to their Samoan extended families

---

9. I thank Toeutu Fa'aleava for this insight (personal communication).

is through these ritual exchanges, making their contributions to these events that much more crucial. Failure to contribute has come to mean failure to be part of the family—an isolation that several people I interviewed had experienced. One of the typical stories I heard was of people who, in their early twenties, decided they would not be contributing to their family's *fa'alavelave*. They often were recently married and wanted to put their resources into their households. As a result, they were gradually cut off from their extended family. Their parents no longer asked them for money, and they were no longer actively involved in the flow of information and activity that surrounds these events. Often, once they had children, or were a bit more settled, they would begin contributing again. Not to contribute was to fail to behave like a Samoan family member—a failure that ultimately makes one not part of a Samoan family, unless you begin contributing again.

The elicitor, too, risks a form of failure because the elicitor's role implicitly involves knowing how much each person can contribute. The very act of requesting the resources carries within it an assumption that this request can be met, that the person does have the resources, partially because the role of elicitor is to be the decision maker about how resources move through the family. Before the introduction of money, this was far more possible. A Samoan migrant in San Francisco with whom I discussed this chapter agreed. He said, "In Samoa, the *matai* can just go outside and count the number of pigs he can use. But here—" and he shrugged. Money, and the potential for concealment that money carries with it, makes a realistic understanding of other people's resources much more difficult to achieve. Nowadays, the elicitor requests money without a strong sense of what is an impossible demand. The elicitor can often be ignorant of what people can afford to donate but is expected to behave as though he or she is knowledgeable.[10]

Meanwhile, as I have discussed earlier, it is in the elicitee's best short-term interests to prevent others from knowing the exact nature of their resources. This subterfuge is quite carefully and meticulously maintained in order to have money in reserve to meet other financial demands, such as

---

10. Some heads of families, as I discussed earlier, avoid this dilemma by asking each family member to give what they can afford. There is, however, an implicit understanding in these cases of what the actual amount should be—such as $200 for a wedding.

rent or phone bills. For the elicitor, the material costs of daily living are less important than maintaining the family pride in a *fa'alavelave*. The elicitee often hides money in various bank accounts, or with trusted friends, so that they can create room to maneuver. Ironically, this can perpetuate the impression for all that the person has tapped into boundless potential resources.[11]

The elicitee often described a mirror image of the elicitor's ignorance of people's resources in my interviews. People would tell me that they didn't know how they were related to the family hosting the wedding or funeral; they just knew they had to contribute. Sometimes they would talk about phone calls they received from parents back in Samoa telling them a wedding in the village was looming. They would send money for that, only to get a phone call a week later asking for money for the wedding again. The parents had decided to donate the first amount to their church instead because the church had just decided to start fund-raising for a new building. Those elicited had a strong sense that they had no understanding of how the money they contributed would be circulated. Not knowing helps create the boundary between these perspectives. The elicitor does not know the elicitee's capitalist resources, and the elicitee does not know the social paths the elicitor will be maintaining.

The Ignorance in the Elicitation

Elicitees often view their elders as outside of the capitalist system and thus as misunderstanding daily life's financial demands. Elicitees attribute this innocence to their local and Samoan-based elders in two basic ways: by discussing how little the elders understood how limited their resources were and how, in Samoa, none of the demands of modern life exist.

---

11. This is exacerbated when the government intervenes and offers various welfare benefits. In these cases, the amount of money people have accessible is obscured because the government is often seen as a bottomless and boundless resource that the person knows how to tap. For a sophisticated discussion of people's perceptions of the state's role as people strive to be capitalist alongside complex Indonesian ceremonial exchanges, see Keane 2001.

People also perpetuate boundaries between the Samoan perspective and a capitalist perspective through moral discourse. They reserve their vigilance and harshest condemnations for those who do not separate capitalist and Samoan exchange principles appropriately. These criticisms would range from complaining about those in powerful positions who acted only in self-interest, accumulating as capitalist agents are supposed to, yet doing this through Samoan exchanges. I used to hear frequent complaints about orators who would go to any *fa'alavelave* they heard of, regardless of whether they were related, and attempt to speak in order to receive the gestures of gratitude from the hosts for attending the ceremony. One New Zealand–raised man I interviewed told me:

> [T]here's a lot of people in Samoan society at the moment, they keep titles and they go to funerals and weddings because they know they can make something out of it, they can get something back for it. That's really common now. It makes me sick. Sometimes when I go to pick up my mum from church, I go in and watch the proceedings. They divvy up this and that. And you see people who have never ever come to that church, they come from the other side of Auckland to be there, and they've got a title and they know they're going to get something. They're going to leave with something.

Just as frequently, I would hear stories about ministers who embezzled money from their congregation. While I heard these stories as nonspecific rumors, the stories dovetailed with church congregations' vigilance in tracing how money was used by the church each month. The anxieties revolved around people who appeared to merge two exchange systems that are supposed to be kept distinct.

My interlocutors' expression of nostalgia for Samoa seemed to be a thinly veiled nostalgia for a time when they were not continually negotiating these tensions between different types of exchange systems. My interlocutors would often tell me that in Samoa, one doesn't need money to survive. If one is hungry, one can simply pick breadfruit or kill a chicken that is running around outside. No one has to pay electricity bills or pay rent. On the Auckland-based 531 PI Fia-Samoa radio call-in program devoted to funerals, one NZ-based caller provided a typical description:

> I went over to Samoa for my brother's funeral. I found the difference is we gather together here and discuss the amount of money and fine mats and

everything—like where he will be buried and which pastor will say the last words. I'm glad that in the old days, when families lost a loved one, most of the expenses came from the land—cows, pigs, fine mats, taro, *taamu* [large tuber], breadfruit, and so on. So it's a small amount of money, like two hundred dollars. Compared with NZ now, Samoans in New Zealand when they do the culture for the funeral, they spend so much. I don't know whether it is because they have a lot of money or they really miss or loved this lost one. They buy so much food and an expensive coffin. But in Samoa in the old days they just wrapped the person in fine mats and then buried him or her. But in here they not only do Samoan culture but also palagi [white] culture. So to me it's very expensive. Our culture is important, but what we are doing here I call too much Samoan culture. Compared with Samoa, they do these things because they had produce from the farm. [translated from Samoan]

When I asked people why they came to the United States or New Zealand, they would tell me it was for the opportunities to send money back home. Clearly these migrants understood that living in Samoa also required money. They are not nostalgic for a place without monetary demands; they are nostalgic for a time when people understood that they had finite resources at their disposal—when their ability to tap into the capitalist exchange system did not make them indexes of boundless resources, with all the demands and financial pressures that go along with that illusion.

Those receiving requests will often practice strategic ignorance, such as ignoring early morning phone calls so that they don't have to send money home to help build the village church. They use small moments of private communicative failures to mitigate family financial pressures. The haphazard communication I witnessed, in which knowing about *fa'alavelave* seemed accidental, allows people some room to decide their own contributions.[12] They must be quite judicious about using various techniques to funnel resources haltingly and gradually into the maw of Samoan exchanges. After all, every failure risks family or community disapproval of not being truly Samoan.

As Samoan migrants gather together the resources necessary to honor people and families through *fa'alavelave,* they often face dilemmas shifting

---

12. See Chua 2009 for another ethnographic example and analysis of the potentially disempowering effects of knowing.

resources from one exchange system to another. At the heart of these social dilemmas is an urgent social need to distinguish between exchange systems, to ensure that Samoan ritual exchanges and capitalist exchanges are
indeed kept separate and distinct, that the cultural and the acultural aren't
perceived as mixing inappropriately. Samoan migrants practice a range of
strategies to establish and maintain the boundaries between cultural and
acultural exchanges within their families. They distinguish sharply between the perspectives and responsibilities of the elicitors and the elicitees,
so that elicitors pay attention to certain kinds of knowledge while elicitees focus on other knowledge. Each develop techniques for managing the
limited resources available to them; techniques that often end up creating
further complications for family members. Ensuring that one is moving
between exchange systems instead of improperly merging exchange systems is an endlessly complicated task.

By focusing on elicitation rather than Samoan exchange, I am analyzing
aspects that my interlocutors are ambivalent about expressing in a public arena such as an academic monograph. As I mentioned before, people
would repeatedly tell me (on discovering I was an anthropologist) both
how much they wanted to honor their family in *fa'alavelave* and how difficult this was. Because I am not Samoan, telling me of their ambivalence
was not a betrayal of their respect and love for their family and Samoan
culture. Everyone spoke to me about the burdens of the Samoan exchange
system—from chiefs and ministers to teenagers and elders. But when I
began to show an early version of this chapter to some of my interlocutors, I was cautioned that I was being too critical of *fa'alavelave*. I was not
properly conveying the pride and support *fa'alavelave* enabled families to
express.[13]

When my interlocutors cautioned me about not presenting the benefits
of *fa'alavelave*—of which there are many—I realized that I am reframing their comments to me about exchanges in a significant way. Eytan
Bercovitch (1994), in his analysis of the relationship between open and hidden exchanges, argues that his focus draws attention to "the way that people
do not so much perpetuate a social order (which can never be realised) as
they perpetuate their relation *to* a social order" (525). I am shifting ground

---

13. My interlocutors also rightly reminded me of several instances in which *matai* and ministers tried to institute broad reforms to curtail the amounts exchanged in *fa'alavelave*.

in a similar way. My interlocutors would discuss their difficulties in perpetuating a Samoan social order *within* the context of capitalist demands on their resources. In my analysis, I have translated their dilemma into one of perpetuating their relation to social orders they experience as distinct and incompatible. In direct contradistinction to their own practices, I am passing over the pride in order to make visible the work of keeping cultural and acultural perspectives distinct.

2

The Moral Economies of Conversion

In navigating two different exchange systems, Samoan migrants are often sorting practices as cultural and acultural at a granular level. In these moments, when capitalism is understood as acultural, it often is also seen as amoral. Capitalism is implicitly counterpoised with being cultural in *fa'alavelave* (Samoan ritual exchanges) in these moments, where being cultural is equated with being moral, loving, and supporting one's family. Yet within Samoan communities, being acultural does not always entail being amoral. Indeed, joining a new, less overtly Samoan church is a common moral, yet putatively acultural, solution to the catch-22s generated by *fa'alavelave*. Samoan migrants will often change their relationships to their local Samoan communities by changing churches, finding Samoan communities that allow them to express their devotion to God in ways they find more appealing. In the process, they are often moving away from certain practices seen as profoundly cultural, yet they no longer take these practices to be moral. They move toward practices they see as aculturally Christian and appropriately moral in a way that participants view as meaningfully different than the Christianity practiced in Samoan church-es.[1] Unlike the dynamic intertwining cultural (and moral) *fa'alavelave* and acultural (and amoral) capitalist exchanges in the previous chapter, Sa-moan migrants who convert see moving away from cultural churches and toward acultural churches as becoming more moral.

In 1830, John Williams from the London Missionary Society brought a new set of practices with global resonances to Samoa in the form of Chris-tianity. Since then, spreading the Christian gospel offered Samoans op-portunities to travel around the Pacific as missionaries under the aegis of the London Missionary Society or the Methodist Church (Lange 1997, 19). In the last fifty years, this penchant for converting other Pacific Island-ers has often led to competition between churches. Samoans continue to convert others and each other, but the conversion is now frequently from one form of Christianity to another. This change has made conversion into a question of what it means to be cultural or acultural from a Samoan perspective. When converting from one form of Christianity to another, Samoans described some relationships they had to Christianity as cultural and other relationships as acultural. Conversion can encourage Samoans to distinguish between being cultural and being moral; it provokes compari-sons that are also critiques of Samoan culture. In this chapter, I will discuss how contemporary conversion requires that Samoans attribute culture, morality, meaning, and meaninglessness anew to various forms of Chris-tian worship. In doing so, they generate reflexive explanations of their per-sonal transformations. I focus on Samoan migrants who join evangelical churches, rejecting Catholicism or more established Protestantism.

In this chapter I am discussing conversions in which Samoans are not re-jecting one set of moral guidelines for another but rather shifting from one form of Christianity to another. While my interlocutors would tell me oc-casionally that people who worship in more established Samoan churches (such as Catholic or Congregational) are not truly Christian but rather are too cultural, this critique seemed based on their assessment of mainline Christian practices and the authenticity of others' beliefs, not a doctrinal difference. What intrigues me most about these conversions is that my interlocutors were not rejecting the content of a former Christianity: many

---

1. See Joel Robbins 2004 for discussion of how global Pentecostalism is often predicated on a break with tradition.

were willing to attend a mainline church in the morning and worshipped in evangelical churches in the afternoon.[2] I argue that they are rejecting the reflexive stance to a moral order that their Samoan church congregation encouraged along with the *fa'alavelave*. Instead, they are adopting a different stance to a Christian moral order, one they consider more valid. Both *fa'alavelave* and neoliberal forms of capitalism will structure certain reflexive stances as moral. People are transitioning between these two different reflexive stances. They are moving between orientations *to* moral orders; they are not moving between two fundamentally different moral orders.

Meaningful Worship

When my interlocutors discussed their decisions to change churches with me, they did not talk about switching moral orientations. While the content of their preoccupations has led me to this analysis, their own voiced concerns were with meaningful expressions of worship. They spoke often about how worship in more mainline churches felt meaningless—that the services were not adequate vehicles for allowing them to convey and experience their strong connection to God. They were suggesting that what they defined as uniquely cultural practices were not paths toward engaging with God. In this chapter, I am arguing that my interlocutors' attributions of meaning and meaninglessness to particular forms of worship are the tangible ways in which they experience their connections to a moral order. They will experience an orientation to a moral order as meaningful if that orientation allows them to structure their practices in ways they find compelling; they experienced orientations to moral orders that do not as meaningless. These were often orientations that they saw as so cultural that it clouded worship, and this distinction enabled them to start framing cultural practices such as ritual exchanges as meaningless. Describing

2. Cluny and La'avasa Macpherson (2001) have written about Samoans who move between churches over a lifetime, leaving the more mainline churches in their late teens and twenties and returning once they have children. They argue that their construction of their own ethnicity is central to this cycle. They also point out, apropos of this chapter, that Samoan migrants' decisions to return to more traditional Samoan churches will often be based on their desire to provide their children with appropriate Samoan contexts.

fa'alavelave as meaningless was not a possibility that was accessible other-
wise. So where I would speak of one's stance toward a moral order, my interlocutors would speak of meaning.

I am departing from other recent scholarship on new religious conversions in the Pacific. The focus in literature on conversion in the Pacific has
been primarily on initial conversions to Christianity, not on how people
choose to move from church to church (Ballard 2000; Barker 1990; Firth
1976; Hefner 1993). Even when looking at conversion between Christian denominations, other analysts have emphasized the ways in which Polynesians
retain precontact spiritual beliefs up until the moment when they convert to
a new form of Christianity by joining a Mormon or an evangelical church
(Ernst 1994; Ramstad 2000). These scholars view conversions as transformations of worldviews, in accordance with Bennetta Jules-Rosette (1975,
135), who describes *conversion* as "a powerful clash resulting from the shift
of one realm of thought and action to another." This is not the perspective
I take here. In this chapter, I am giving weight to the fact that the people I
interviewed had been Christian prior to their conversion experience. They
were not switching moral orders but rather changing the ways in which
they related to the moral order in which they participated. I am also departing from other scholarly perspectives by focusing on the Christianities
my interlocutors left behind, instead of uncovering the lingering vestiges of
non-Christian spiritual beliefs.[3] In this sense, I am responding to Joel Robbins' call to look at the ways in which Pentecostal religions can be socially
constructed to offer discontinuities and to critically examine both continuity
and discontinuity (see Robbins 2003). Robbins points out that Pentecostal
believers often view their faith in terms of discontinuities, which is at odds
with scholars' focus on continuities in traditions. He calls for analyses that
examine how people imagine and use ruptures as well as perceived continuities. For Samoan migrants who converted, the rupture they were imagining
was an incomplete break with culture. They were not leaving behind being
Samoan, but they were leaving behind the ways a more traditional Samoan
church structured how people could express their Samoan commitments.

When my interlocutors convert, they are responding to the ways in
which the moral is created in the various church-based moral economies

---

3. See John Barker 2001 for a direct critique of this tendency in Ernst 2000.

in which they engage. My interlocutors are not only leaving churches, they are also leaving behind ways of presenting themselves as moral beings through complex economic Samoan exchanges (see also Besnier 2011 for an account of a similar dynamic in Tonga). When they enter new congregations, they learn new ways to be reflexively linked to moral economies. At the same time, my interlocutors would attribute meaninglessness to the ways that the church economies that they rejected are experienced by others as moral; that is, they were realigning their understandings of what it meant to be cultural and acultural. These shifts in meaning and morality were often also shifts in reflexivity—people were learning to carve out different personhoods through these conversions as well. What was at stake in conversion for my interlocutors was not the type of doctrine they believed but the type of moral self they fashioned. Thus the meaninglessness that my interlocutors found in mainline Samoan churches had little to do with texts and everything to do with how best to practice Christianity, which included how best to demonstrate their faith.

The Accidental Fieldworker

I did my research for this chapter unintentionally, in the pursuit of other questions. The majority of these interviews took place while I was interviewing couples in mixed marriages to collect accounts of how Samoan families experience cultural difference. I would ask people at the end of the interview if they knew of anyone else I should interview. This technique generated its own dynamic in my fieldwork, providing entry to a community of people, all of whom knew each other. For a period of three or four months, I was interviewing around twenty couples who attended evangelical Christian churches. After several of these interviews, I learned that a good question for eliciting complex life stories was asking how they had received the Lord into their life. It would trigger a narrative, well-rehearsed and illuminating. I would learn about conversions, about how their lives profoundly changed in response to a powerful spiritual insight. I would also learn a tremendous amount about their lives in general. I was always clear that I did not share their faith. I am Jewish, which was a curiosity for them, but also made me into a possible convert. While I don't think that this was necessarily at stake in every, or even many, of these interviews, it was an undercurrent (largely because in the evangelical Christian imaginary, giving testimony about receiving Christ into ones' life often occurs in an enunciative space of nonbelievers [see Crapanzano 1994, 871; Harding 2000, 39]). But I was a single-minded interviewer, who cared only about the nuances of families. I did not appreciate what people were trying to tell me about how relating to Christian precepts from an evangelical perspective changed them. In this chapter, I am responding to the conversion element in the stories that I collected and the people I spoke with, albeit in hindsight.

Most of the couples I interviewed attended a Pentecostal church that met every Sunday in a benefactor's commercial gym. Meeting in a gym, surrounded by mirrors and nylon stuffed mats, created a literal subtext of muscular Christianity. People dressed casually, sometimes in T-shirts and jeans, in contrast to the more formal attire that Samoan migrants would wear to other churches (see also Besnier 2011). This church was a culturally mixed congregation, although the founding families and most active members were people from Samoa or married to people from Samoa.[4] While I was doing fieldwork, this could sporadically elicit criticism that the church was too Samoan. Those running the church were often connected through family ties—the pastor at the time was an Australian whose mother-in-law was a very influential Samoan woman and a prominent figure in several of the conversion stories I collected. Her children and relatives were also active church members. There were many young families, and there was a cadre of single people, many of whom were evaluating each other as potential spouses. Of the Samoan migrants who attended, many described themselves as New Zealand–raised Samoan. The church also met late in the afternoon, allowing people to attend other churches. While the church itself was in West Auckland and drew most of its congregation from surrounding neighborhoods, people would also travel from Central Auckland and even forty-five minutes to an hour from South Auckland to worship there. Several of the members I interviewed were part of an emerging Samoan socioeconomic group supported by neoliberal government policies that privileged culturally appropriate training, working for job training,

---

4. This strong Samoan contingent might be unusual for congregations Samoans choose to join. Both Cluny Macpherson and Melani Anae found in their research that the converts they spoke to prefer attending evangelical churches with less of a Samoan influence.

and other government-sponsored programs for assisting people who are unemployed. Three Samoan members of the All-Blacks, New Zealand's national rugby team, attended while I was doing research. It was a congregation full of people learning how to negotiate their surrounding systems successfully and teaching others how to do so as well.

While many of the interviews I collected were from members of this church, my collection of conversion narratives was by no means limited to this one church. The people I spoke with were limited, however, by age. With a few exceptions, I did not gather these narratives from anyone over fifty, and for the most part the people I interviewed were in their mid-twenties to late thirties. As in chapter 1, I was interviewing people in the age range most likely to be impacted strongly by family and church financial demands, and least likely to be gaining clear-cut benefits from participating in family and church exchanges.

Rational Choice or Revelation?

The narratives I was collecting operated for me at two levels, and it is the contradictions between these levels that I hope to reconcile through the course of this chapter. People were offering me heartfelt and strongly emotional stories of experiences that I kept rereading through a sociological lens. They would tell me stories about how they had experienced a strong physical connection to Christ at the moment of becoming born-again, stories such as this one:

> The following year I actually once again went with my cousin and his wife who were in the same kind of movement to their church, and had the same kind of service, like clapping and chanting and singing and dancing and speaking in tongues. And I was just standing there and, and I thought. And I didn't know what to say, what I said was I think I prayed two things like— Please God, or Please Jesus. And suddenly this power that just came, it was just over my head and all the way down. It was like a bucket of water, it was just very cleansing. My whole being was like transforming into things, it was really dynamic.

It is possible to read this account in terms of anxieties over group membership or as a ritual of initiation. But that focus does not address the other elements of my interlocutor's experience: the sense of cleansing and transformation in her encounter with the spiritual. Other anthropologists have discussed this dilemma, most notably Edith Turner in her revision of Victor Turner's account of healing among the Ndembu (Turner 1992). Edith Turner was arguing that perhaps there were forces to be accounted for in healing ceremonies that transcended functionalist arguments of newly created social harmonies. Others have written about instances in which their analytical frameworks were not only at odds with their informants' beliefs but insulting to them (see Brettell 1993). I experienced the same tensions time and time again as I discussed with my interlocutors their reasons for becoming evangelical Christians. The sociological explanations I suggested were not welcome to the people I spoke with in New Zealand and the United States, and they often gently told me that the motivations I attributed were not people's motivations at all.

So what motivations did I persistently insist on attributing to why people converted? I fear that my explanations never revolved around revelation or faith—my first mistake. The explanation I used to offer my interlocutors in the field when discussing these conversions between Christianities all presumed that people were acting as rational choice actors. Moreover, I was suggesting that it was economically advantageous for people not to attend churches my interlocutors would describe as more traditionally Samoan, such as EFKS (Ekalesia Fa`apotopotoga Kerisiano of Samoa, originally London Missionary Society) or the Catholic Church. People who attended evangelical churches would not have to contribute as much money or as often as those who belonged to EFKS, Catholic, or Congregational churches. My interlocutors would politely but firmly reject these explanations, and they would occasionally discuss instead the meaningless worship they perceived to be present in these churches. My explanation was too limited to explain the transformations conversion enables—the new allocations of meaning and meaninglessness in how people experience their relationship to a Samoan moral order.

Knowing Pride When You See It

My first encounter with Samoan migrants who attended non-mainline churches occurred during one of my first interviews with mixed-marriage couples in Auckland. I was interviewing a twenty-four-year-old

New Zealand–raised woman, Lotu, who grew up in the Seventh Day Adventist (SDA) Church. Sara, her mother, was present, and so the conversation included a generational perspective. We chatted about the role cultural differences had played in Lotu's relationship with her partner, who was from Tonga. Lotu told me with animation how much she had suffered for being the daughter-in-law in a Tongan family, how her husband's sisters had complete authority to take any of her daughter's clothes, and so on. Later, when Sara drove me home, she turned to me and asked me what one word I thought would have summed up the whole interview. I had not so long ago taken my doctoral qualifying exams—one word answers did not leap easily to mind. I muttered something about the dynamics of kinship, and she glanced at me, tolerant but bemused. "No," she said when I finally stopped floundering in academic phrases, "power—it is all about power." Sara was right, her daughter had been telling me the entire time the ways in which her Tongan in-laws invoked tradition to control her behavior. From that moment on, whenever Sara summed up a situation for me, I always listened very carefully to her.

During the months that I went to this SDA church, Sara would occasionally ask me what I was discovering. And then, each time, she would ask me if I had come to the conclusion that Samoans are a very proud people. *Pride,* for Sara, was as weighty a word as power. I started to listen closely to what work "pride" was doing for Samoans—aside from contributing the slogan "Samoan Pride" to T-shirts festooned with muscle-bound tattooed Samoan men. As I listened more carefully, I began to notice that pride, and its ever-present conceptual partner, shame, was one of a small number of motivations people consistently attributed to each other. And pride was one of the few motivations (among the ever-available options of respect, love, desire for power, desire for people, selfishness, and so on) that Samoan migrants used to explain other people's commitments to family or communities when they were expressed through *fa'alavelaves* (ritual exchanges). Pride was the word people used to explain others' emotional motivations and moral engagements with *fa'alavelave.*

The Moral in Samoan Moral Economy

When Sara asked me whether I noticed how much pride motivated Samoans, she was asking me about people's commitments to a Samoan moral economy—commitments about which many of my interlocutors had mixed feelings. She was rejecting the reflexive position one must take to see that the *fa'alavelave* occurring in church contexts are part of a Samoan moral economy. Here I am discussing *moral economy* in a way that might be unfamiliar. Scholars often use the term moral economy to refer to the moral assumptions that underlie economic practices (Scott 1976; Thompson 1971, 1991). Frequently these moral assumptions are not visible or clearly articulated until people are confronted with the possibilities of alternative economic practices that violate their moral principles.[5] I am suggesting that in order to act on the precepts of a moral economy, one must assume a particular reflexive stance defined in situ by the moral economy. From the perspective of someone rejecting the assumptions of a Samoan moral economy, the reflexive stance rejected is discussed as one of pride.

When people from Samoa would describe to me why they personally contribute when there is a *fa'alavelave,* they would invariably cast it in terms of a strong sense of obligation and affection for their family. When describing other people, they might discuss it in terms of pride, as Sara did. But when discussing their own reasons, it was invariably in the language of love and responsibility. To be part of a Samoan family is to be committed to making the family's strength and status visible by contributing money, food, and fine mats to one's church and to *fa'alavelave.* The family reveals its capacity in these moments and expresses both pride and *alofa* (respectful love) for one's family. So there are strong moral valences attached toward contributing to *fa'alavelave;* when one contributes to the church, one is revealing love for God and family in one fell swoop. And through this public ritual, one is also affirming the family's position vis-à-vis other families in the community. This combination of *alofa* and pride was frequently described to me as a potent motivating force.

Moral Exchange, Meaningful Economy

In this section, I sketch how migration has affected the *fa'alavelave* that take place in churches. I outline the ways in which a contextual morality is fashioned within migrant Samoan communities by looking at how

---

5. See E. P. Thompson (1971) for an account of how food riots in the sixteenth through eighteenth centuries were responses by peasants to violations of their moral expectations of farmers' and millers' economic practices.

church exchanges allow people to make their moral fiber visible. Churches enable people to reveal unities at two different levels—both as a congregation and as members of families that constitute a congregation. Here I am pointing to a distinction between levels of scale constituted by exchange. When people operate (or act) as a congregation, their attention tends to be occupied by supporting their minister, building new churches, paying off church mortgages through monthly contributions, and contributing to other churches. At stake in these exchanges is peoples' ability to demonstrate what their congregation can accomplish together. Peoples' financial obligations are not limited to their own church's building. Congregations are also often engaging in historically complex exchanges with other local churches. Ministers visit other congregations frequently and must be treated with a proper respect that includes gifts of food, money, and fine mats. In addition, when other churches consecrate their new buildings, there are often costly financial obligations when participating in those celebrations. For example, while I was doing fieldwork in Auckland in 1997, the EFKS Otara church rebuilt its church buildings. The all-day celebration included contributions by churches from all over Auckland that ranged from $10,000 NZ to $75,000 NZ per congregation. These contributions are collected because of the pressure to contribute to support ones' church's reputation that is created by an imagined outside gaze constituted by larger Samoan communities.

Belonging to a church also means responding to one's own congregation as an imagined judging gaze. Families compete within a congregation to demonstrate their relative strength as well. This occurs in several ways, but most visibly toward the end of every Sunday church service when a deacon reads the lists of who contributed and the amount. People don't always contribute as a family or a household. In one of the churches I attended, women contributed one week, men the next. Yet the names for the most part reference households' resources, not individuals' resources. This is the most predictable contribution one has to make—belonging to a church also involves contributing at fellow congregants' weddings, funerals, birthdays, and so on in a competitive context that can quickly escalate.

In moving between moral economies, Samoan migrants are moving between church communities that engage differently with Samoan ritual exchanges. Church communities' diasporic practices of *fa'alavelave* have largely been formed by histories of migration. *Fa'alavelave* in general have become a central ritual for migrants to express their connection to their family and to Samoa. The initial migrants' youth was a large factor in how *fa'alavelave* after migration evolved. As I mentioned earlier, the first people to migrate from Samoa in large numbers were predominantly young men and women who had scholarships or opportunities at manual labor jobs (Pitt and Macpherson 1974). Their families chose who would migrate by carefully assessing who would be likely to help other family members, both by sending money back home and by assisting others to migrate to New Zealand or the United States (Macpherson and Macpherson 2009). Families would choose members who were still at a stage of life in which they were supposed to labor physically to serve the family and who were not yet responsible for making decisions about larger family strategies. The new migrants suddenly found themselves in an unexpected position of autonomy, able to decide how they would spend money or what they would contribute to exchanges occurring in their new communities.

When migrants first began to arrive in the 1950s, they were far more concerned with sending resources back to Samoa then in building demanding exchange networks within New Zealand or the United States. According to my interviews, when migrants initially began establishing migrant communities, they were not actively participating in *fa'alavelave*. The first large-scale exchanges began within the newly formed Pacific Island churches. It even took several years before fine mats, an integral part of Samoan exchanges, made their way over to New Zealand or the United States. While migrants began building exchange networks from within the churches and with family members who had also migrated, the depth of historical relationships represented by the exchanges was far shallower then in Samoa. People were often commemorating relationships forged over the past decade or so, rather than over generations. Their parents back home in Samoa were determining how resources were to be allocated for the exchanges that resonated with generational depth. As I pointed out in chapter 1, often people wouldn't know how the money that they were sending back home would be used, so they could not easily shoulder the burden of subsequent exchanges based on these transactions.

This initial shift created changes in the ways in which migrants use *fa'alavelave* to express their connections with their family even to this day.

Just as with knowledge transmission for my interlocutors raised outside of Samoa, parents often become the primary vehicle through which migrants stay connected to the Samoan exchange system. The links between Samoa and New Zealand or the United States are often carried out through a parent-child link. A village back in Samoa will decide that it needs to build a new church and ask each family in the village to contribute money toward this goal. The parents will start calling their children overseas, asking them to send some money for the church. The children may not feel connected to the village itself; they might not have lived there for twenty years.[6] But because their parents are asking them for money, they will send money back to Samoa. Samoan-raised migrants still have first cousins and siblings in Samoa, but often many of the close relatives in their generation will have migrated as well. As people become second- or third-generation migrants, the majority of *fa'alavelave* they contributed to were in New Zealand or the United States. Even Samoan-raised migrants often have the majority of their siblings living overseas, so their parents are often their main connection to Samoa. While they continue to remit, and constantly travel back and forth between Samoa and New Zealand or the United States, they also are funneling more and more of their resources into their local exchange networks.

After migration, people did not re-create village hierarchies by living in the same neighborhood or even using villages as a basis for association until the late 1990s. Church congregations began to be the primary site for determining relative worth within the local Samoan communities. When sending money back to Samoa, their contributions were merged into a display of family strength in the village. The overseas Samoans' resources are sustaining a nostalgic unity, not the one they currently try to make visible in their daily lives. However, during *fa'alavelave* held in local churches, there would be a public display of the connections created through their contributions—their contributions would be publicly acknowledged in rituals in ways that were rendered invisible overseas. In short, for Samoan migrants, mainline Samoan churches have become the primary site through which people can enact being moral Samoans through *fa'alavelave*. Thus when

---

6. According to people I interviewed in Wellington, it is only in the early 1990s that Samoans in New Zealand have begun fundraising for their village back in Samoa as a whole group. Until then, Samoans were either raising money as a family or as a church.

they are converting from one church to another, they are also moving from one form of local exchange network to another, and also between church-based moral economies.

As I described in chapter 1, Samoan migrants often straddle two contradictory perspectives. From the capitalist perspective, being involved with *fa'alavelave* can seem overwhelming: one has to contribute substantial amounts of money at an unpredictable rate. It is difficult to plan or budget—counter to the guiding principles that capitalist perspectives often demand that people use to manage themselves and their resources. Funerals or sudden weddings can occur at any time, and people cannot easily anticipate how much they will need to contribute from week to week or month to month.[7] But from the perspective of Samoan ritual exchange, it is difficult not to exchange. The reasons to give are emotionally charged. Not giving is a sign of not wanting to support one's family, of not wanting to be part of the complex emotional connections of familial affection made visible through exchange.

People from Samoa reading this may think I am blaming *fa'asamoa* (literally, the Samoan way) for particular financial conundrums that Samoan migrants experience. This is not the case. In chapter 1, I pointed out that the problems arise because people are operating within two exchange systems: capitalism and Samoan ritual exchanges. It would be easy to blame Samoan ritual exchanges for placing people in particular traps. But this would disguise the pragmatic ways in which capitalism in New Zealand and the United States does not encourage people to support their family through familiar Samoan avenues. It is not *fa'alavelave* per se that are the problem; it is negotiating two contradictory economic systems at the same time.

Converting Out of Context

Converting to being a born-again Christian (or less mainline Christian) reformulates one's relationship to both of these economic perspectives. When people from Samoa convert from one form of Christianity to another, they are most often leaving a church more involved with Samoan

---

7. As I discussed in chapter 1, families will often establish a pool of money reserved for *fa'alavelave* to which every family member contributes a small sum weekly or biweekly. This creates a cushion in case of sudden and unexpected *fa'alavelave*.

ritual exchanges and entering churches with strong injunctions against these ritual exchanges. This was particularly true of the first wave of reformist Christianity to be adopted by people from Samoa, such as Seventh Day Adventistism or Mormonism. To belong to the Seventh Day Adventist Church is to refuse to worship on Sunday, to avoid pork, dancing, tattooing, and, most important, to refuse to exchange fine mats. Born-again Christians have similar injunctions against engaging in Samoan ritual exchange, although dancing and eating pork are not taboo. Significantly, most of the churches will not tithe publicly; the church service does not approach a conclusion by having a deacon call out the amounts specific people have donated. Several of my interlocutors would stress how important it was to them that they attended a church with anonymous collections. One evangelical minister offered the following comparison:

> I found out in the islands, I observed it myself as a young man, on a Sunday every month they used to take up the love offering for the *faifeau* [church minister]. The way it is conducted in the church is just like money changers in the temple that Jesus threw out. Now the secretary would go up to the front of the church, the old faifeau sitting there half-asleep, fat stomach [laughs] and I am not being critical because I could have been caught up in it only the Lord has changed my life and my whole outlook. And then the secretary says, "Right, today is the love offering for the faifeau. I would like you to give generously for God's servant." And so the family gets up and goes up—one hundred dollars. And then the next family goes up. And they announce it. The family of John Groendahl [a pseudonym] have now contributed one hundred dollars for the love offering for the minister. And the next family goes up, and they say now Ilana's family has now contributed two hundred dollars to the minister. And the next thing, this guy John sends up the kid and he whispers, "My dad said to add another one hundred fifty to the offering." It is now that the Groendahl family will increase their offering to...It's like an auction. And in our church here, we have offerings; we call it a free will offering. We have bags and nobody knows what the next person puts in. And we emphasize to the folk that what you put in, some people are able to put in more than others, those who can not afford it, don't you feel obligated. You are just as much a part of this church.

In this minister's account of Samoan giving, he mentions conversion, pointing out that this form of giving would have been meaningful for him still if the Lord had not intervened and changed his whole outlook. Notice also that it is not giving to the church that is the problem for my interlocutor but rather how public, and thus how competitive, this giving is in mainline Samoan churches. My interlocutor was very aware that public giving ensured that church members would give more than they had anticipated giving. From his perspective, mainline Samoan churches were arenas of evaluation and competition expressed through supposedly more traditional Samoan ritual exchanges. These less traditional churches create new venues through which Samoans can demonstrate their moral character, venues that do not require public displays of giving. This minister and my other interlocutors were pointing to the fact that these churches do not compel people to negotiate capitalism and Samoan ritual exchange. Instead, the churches were encouraging their congregants to restructure their relationships to Samoan ritual exchanges, and thus to Samoan culture.

I interviewed a Mormon couple—the wife from a Samoan family; the husband from a European New Zealand family—who were quite explicit about the costs families had to pay when contributing to *fa'alavelave* and the escapes the new Christian churches could provide. In the following conversation, this couple discusses ritual exchanges as "culture," providing what I mentioned earlier as a common focus on pride as a principal motivation:

THOMAS: I work in South Auckland, and I see it everyday. I see how Polynesian families are just struggling to cope with the social ills of that area.

SINA: And it doesn't help when the culture, when their culture, when some families' culture is the main focus of their life. I am not kidding; I have seen it. And it is so sad. Because their children get neglected—so much pride and they just give, give, give and the children suffer.

THOMAS: There should be an even balance of everything as far as I am concerned. But some families, the main priority is their culture, their church perhaps. We believe that there should be a fair balance of everything.

SINA: We support my culture. If my family needs help, like if one of my brothers gets married, or someone goes on a mission, or a relative dies, we give what we can afford. But my parents don't—before they used to, eh?— but they don't put pressure on us. Now they don't. They are really adapting to the [Mormon] church culture.

Culture becomes a slippery term in this conversation, moving from referencing what it means to be Samoan to what it means to be Mormon. For this couple, Mormonism provided them with a perspective that encouraged focusing their resources on their nuclear family rather than their extended family (see Gordon 1990 for discussion of this process among Mormon Tongan families). In addition, Mormonism also changed their relationship to the Samoan wife's parents, who had recently converted.

Because of this restructuring, it may be compelling to read this conversion as a movement toward becoming a rational choice actor. Samoan migrants are doing what is economically feasible. Caught in a system in which they must spread their financial resources too thin, they turn to newer forms of Christianity to be able to continue engaging in producing community that feels Samoan but without the financial costs of producing a community structured along Samoan exchange principles. From a perspective formed by capitalist impulses, it is a compelling reason—switching forms of worship to reduce the contributions that more mainline Samoan churches seem to demand.

I want to suggest that the change people are experiencing is a different one: they are not becoming rational choice actors as much as becoming different kind of moralists. They are choosing to move away from a faith that is exhibited to a faith that is emoted. People address this shift in their comparisons between mainline and evangelical churches. Most frequently, my interlocutors would compare the styles of worship: They noted that in mainline churches people sat formally and quietly; in evangelical churches, the worship would be exuberant, complete with energetic singing and movement (see Tiatia 1998, 160–165, and Besnier 2011, 205–230, for comparisons of styles of worship). The difference between these styles of worship can be described as a distinction between being and achieving. In more mainline churches, people are being worshipful without revealing the effort that goes into producing faith. In evangelical churches, people are revealing the effort, they are making visible the labor that goes into making a worshipful self.

In addition, what people are rejecting in moving away from the mainline Samoan churches is a morality based on public displays of family strength and public evaluations in church contexts. My interlocutors were rejecting the importance of others' gazes as the guarantee of moral Christian behavior. When rejecting this morality, they begin experiencing it as meaningless. Bradd Shore has argued that others' gazes are a crucial moral restraint for Samoans, as a consequence of the Samoan concept of personhood. He argues that for Samoans morality is sociocentric, and human nature is viewed as instinctual and socially destructive. As he writes:

"Perhaps most significantly, village law and authority are understood to protect people from themselves—from passions and desires that, uncontained by culture and customary authority, would lead to moral and social chaos" (118). For Shore, the cultural context determines how people from Samoa will behave, not an internally cohesive intentionality. Notice that *culture* here is equivalent to morality. Shore argues that the Samoans believe that motivation is only partially linked to the actor's internal qualities or decisions. "Samoans commonly talk about actions and feelings as if the body were a decentralized agglomeration of discrete parts, each imbued with its own will" (173). The social context determines which part of the conglomerate Samoan self will be made explicit. One of the consequences is that people in public might appear to behave in ways that dramatically contradict their private behavior.

A corollary to this ethnographic claim is that people from Samoa hold moral selves to be public, and potentially amoral selves private. Bradd Shore describes this as the Samoan link between knowledge and responsibility. He argues that for Samoans, a misdeed is not a misdeed until the person is publicly held responsible: "private or purely personal knowledge of one's own actions is not sufficient grounds for responsibility for them. Knowledge of one's actions must be public to some extent for one to be responsible" (1982, 175). An action is neither good nor bad until it has been judged so by others. From a Samoan perspective, *meaning*—or in Shore's case *morality*—must be coproduced (see also Duranti 1994). There is no such thing as a private morality; morality exists only when one is judged by others.

Evangelical Christianity offers Samoan migrants an appealing alternative to this form of morality: a church in which the main focus is the labor of self-making. One of my interlocutors was direct and pithy about this transformation, saying: "We kind of had to reevaluate who we were. But I think Christianity does that to you, it forces you to reevaluate, renew your mind. It causes you to stop, think, look, and renew your mind." These evangelical churches differ from mainline churches in one aspect that has become crucial for my interlocutors—instead of a context in which one should not make visible the labor that goes into making oneself moral, they provide a context in which this labor is glorified. In mainline churches, people are criticized for not obeying the contextual cues, for not fulfilling their roles properly. In evangelical churches, they are commended for precisely the behavior that drew condemnation in their previous churches—the *effort* to be good.

Born-again Christians present their conversion experiences time and time again as a move away from a morality based on a Samoan cultural context, although they don't describe it as such, preferring to describe the conversion as moving away from a meaningless form of worship toward a more meaningful form. They are viewing cultural practices such as ritual exchange as spiritually meaningless. They would tell me that people went to Samoan mainline churches to gossip and compete with everyone else, not to worship. Fashioning meaninglessness is also refashioning context. In the moment of labeling a more mainline form of Samoan Christian worship meaningless, the Samoan converts are discarding the claims to a context-dependent morality in favor of a morality based largely on a notion of a consistent and self-monitoring person. The moral meaninglessness that they discover or learn to recognize in a particular form of worship is a meaninglessness emergent from the ways in which Samoans imagine themselves as reflexive and reflexively moral because they joined a more acultural church. In a more mainline Samoan church, the onus is on the production of morality through the demonstration of familial strength and piety or proper behavior. The focus is entirely on the external presentation, a match between contextual demands and appearance. In the born-again churches, the creation of meaning occurs in a different way, through one's reflexive management of oneself as a moral being.[8]

At stake is not the content of the moral beliefs but rather the moral stance itself. When people from Samoa convert from one form of Christianity to another, they do not learn that new behaviors have become immoral. Rather, they learn a new reflexive stance toward being Christian. They no longer are showing the strength of their commitment through exchange but through monitoring the self. They are also moving from what they understand to be Samoan culturally specific Christianity to an acultural Christianity. One interviewee explained to me the problems with Samoan churches as a critique of a contextual moral self.

---

8. It is no accident that several of the people I interviewed were also engaged in teaching other people how to transform themselves into consistent and manageable selves for the job market by running job-training programs.

JANET: He [Sione, her husband] doesn't want to go to a Samoan church.

SIONE: There is a different way that I understand and the way that they understand what it is all about. How to take the Word into yourself, that's what's different. How to put it? In the way I take it, in a European way, it's really deep in me and also it's really serious. In the Christian way of fellowship or worshipping God, it is doing a lot to feed the Holy Spirit in people or in myself. And in Samoa—I haven't been to a Samoan church in a long time—They are only going to church on Sunday for two or three hours to listen to the minister, and that's it. Oh, and Sunday school for the kids. No program to feed the Holy Spirit, no support. That's why they only have the Spirit in themselves on Sunday. And then they walk out and the next day they go back the same way they are.

Sione is criticizing the lack of context through which people can demonstrate their Christian faith. According to him (and not in my experience) in Samoan churches, people must be visibly moral only on Sundays. For this Samoan man, the conversion was a movement toward understanding how to be moral in a new way, one that confirmed a form of meaninglessness on to previous ways of finding moral certainty.

Peter Stromberg (1990) discusses the ways in which conversion can serve to create a coherent self, resolving people's previous emotional contradictions:

> The conversion narrative, like the ritual, induces a sort of "solidarity," in this case a solidarity of motives. The conversion narrative enables the believer to forge a sense of coherence by using the ideological language to embrace intentions that, as the analysis has shown, persist in spite of being denied. It is this sense of coherence that signals, both to the believer and to the observer, a transformed identity. (54)

Stromberg specifically describes how identities that were previously experienced as meaningless become meaningful through the conversion (1990, 53). I am arguing for a cultural specificity to peoples' conversion experiences. By shifting morality from its social construction to an internal management of emotions, and demonstration through emotions, Samoan migrants are moving from having morality defined through contextual "cultural" selves to having morality defined through continuous selves.

The sermons in evangelical churches were often narratives framed in terms of acquiring tools by which to manage oneself. The stories captured my interlocutors' imagination; even the Samoan migrants I spoke with who went to more mainline churches on a regular basis found this aspect of evangelical Christianity appealing. I accompanied two men, who regularly attended their family's mainline churches on Sundays, to hear a visiting evangelical minister from Korea. The visiting preacher was popular enough to fill a large church hall and the huge tent behind. We watched on a large screen as the minister told the audience an inspirational story about a woman who came to him one day seeking advice. She told him that she prayed constantly, but God was not answering her prayers. The preacher asked her what she was praying for, and she replied that she wanted a husband. The preacher wondered if she prayed with any specificity, and the woman replied that she did not. So the preacher told her that if she wanted something, she should pray in detail. She should develop a list of the characteristics she wanted—a thoughtful man, a teacher, a good Christian, and so on. Then, with a list of ten attributes she wanted in a husband, she should pray for precisely that person, and God would provide. She followed his advice, and the next time he visited that town, she was married to a man who matched her wish list. This story, one of several similar stories the minister told, occupied my two Samoan interlocutors for the ride home. The driver turned enthusiastically to his friend as we were heading across a long bridge into the city: "This is what you need to do. You want a wife, you should come up with a list of exactly what you want and start praying for that." What evangelical churches offered were clear and concrete guidelines for how to develop a regulated self and templates for how to be a reflexive self—guidelines for how to think of oneself as an emotional, and often powerfully emotional, person with needs, all of which could still be constructed in a moral valence.

In a Samoan context, morality is usually linked to social contexts rather than to internal impulses, and one's sense of morality is created by others' gazes rather than by a consistent self. Diaspora makes this more complicated. After all, a Samoan morality based on social context requires two elements that are increasingly missing in a Samoan diaspora: being culturally knowledgeable about the cues and guidelines that others' gazes provide, and being in appropriate performative contexts.[9] When Samoan migrants convert to evangelical churches, some of these pressures are removed. They are no longer concerned with being good Samoan Christians as much as they are with practicing how to be good Christians (see Taule'ale'ausumai 1990). Visible effort is irrelevant from a mainline Samoan Christian perspective but valued as meaningful from an evangelical perspective. As a consequence, others' gazes cease to be as relevant as guides to morality; instead my interlocutors wanted to be moral by fashioning and experiencing a faith-filled self.

The transition implied in conversion from one form of Christianity to another is not a movement between Christian principles but a movement between moral economies. Moral economies are not only guidelines for how best to exchange; they also entail the proper stances for being and revealing one's morality. While I have analyzed the stances as reflexive connections to moral orders, my interlocutors would discuss conversion in terms of meaning, of moving from meaningless forms of worship to meaningful ones.

At the same time, they were organizing meaning in the contexts of the cultural and the acultural. Conversion offered a way to distinguish between Samoan culture and morality, creating the possibility that the acultural was moral as well. This goes against common scholarly understandings of the acultural as the site of the modern, the universal, as traditionless. In this case, being acultural was located in a particular set of local practices, admittedly ones with claims for a more global reach (see Robbins 2004). The local effect of this moral acultural venue was to provide those who converted with a chance to disentangle from certain obligations while still following moral precepts. My interlocutors found the moral compasses that more mainline Samoan churches defined as culture increasingly difficult to follow. As a result, they turned to a Christianity that required a different reflexive stance to a moral order. In these cases, conversion was not about the content of one's faith but about the way of being faithful— not about principles but about personhood.

---

9. Samoan youth raised overseas often become icons of the ways in which migration has produced these tensions. It is not surprising that many converts to evangelical churches grew up outside of Samoa.

Part II

Part II Introduction

SOME POLITICAL AND HISTORICAL CONTEXT

I began my fieldwork with Samoan migrants in San Francisco in 1998 after spending a year and a half with Samoan migrant communities in New Zealand. Soon after I began volunteering at the National Office of Samoan Affairs (NOSA) in San Francisco, I saw how different it was to be a Samoan migrant talking about Samoan culture in the United States instead of in New Zealand. I was helping my fellow workers at NOSA to host a meeting between a representative from San Francisco's Department of Human Services (DHS) and the other Samoan community-based organizations in the area. It was my first opportunity in the United States to observe Samoan community workers talking with an official from the U.S. welfare system. I had been in New Zealand just two months earlier, where I met migrants who were advocating for Samoan culture in a myriad of ways: They produced handbooks explaining their cultural background for the government departments in which they worked, successfully advocated for culturally appropriate family conferences for juvenile offenders, and established

Samoan-run and Samoan culture-specific mental health clinics and domestic violence shelters. In New Zealand, "culturespeak" was vibrant and frequent (Goldsmith 2003). I was learning on a daily basis how much my New Zealand experience was shaping my expectations in California.

Tim, the DHS representative, had arranged the meeting with three Samoan organizations in the Bay area a week earlier: NOSA, Samoan Community Development Center, and Soul'd Out Productions. No one was quite sure what his agenda was. Did he know how tenuously cordial and fundamentally antagonistic the heads of these organizations were toward each other as they battled to represent Samoan communities in government contexts? Was this an overt attempt on DHS's part to heal rifts within the Samoan community, or was this simply another of DHS's recent well-meaning attempts at community outreach?

The mystery of Tim's agenda soon revealed itself. Tim's approach was to treat the Samoan organizations as all equally invested in helping their community deal with the complications for families created by recent neoliberal federal policies. He was using this meeting to explain some of the innovative programs DHS were developing in response to the then recent welfare-to-work legislation. As he explained one of these new projects in detail, I was getting more and more uneasy. Since 1996, the U.S. federal government had been putting pressure on the various social service departments to reunify families torn apart by substance abuse and/or child abuse in a more timely fashion. City social workers no longer were guaranteed eighteen months to mend the rifts. Now they could be faced with a six-month deadline to document that the family was showing improvements or else the child would be placed in foster care. Tim was enthusiastic about a novel way to circumvent this deadline: creating governmentally engineered extended families. Specially trained families would adopt a single parent and child pair who were struggling to reform enough in six months to a court's satisfaction. The families would receive larger apartments in state housing projects and some financial support, and, in return, they would take care of a mother and her child. Because the mother and child would technically be under one roof, they would be "reunified" under the adopting family's watchful eyes. While Tim continued unfurling this new plan, no mention of culturally appropriate placement slipped into his descriptions.

Largely because of my experiences in New Zealand, I kept waiting for the reassurance that Tim was concerned about a family's cultural background. I thought that he would feel compelled to discuss how DHS would guarantee cultural sensitivity when he was speaking to community organizations that existed in part to offer cultural expertise. Even stranger, from my perspective, none of the community workers in the meeting seemed inclined to probe this issue. Finally, too curious to stay quiet, I asked Tim whether families would be matched with deference to their cultural backgrounds. I was puzzled that his answer was "no, absolutely not." He explained that families could be matched only using race-blind criteria, but this was designed to ensure equal treatment. Tim explained that legally they could not pay attention to race or ethnicity when manufacturing these social relations. I asked about culture; Tim replied with a discussion of race. With this substitution, racial equality and cultural sensitivity were placed at loggerheads with each other, with racial equality made the priority.

Racial equality was not the only category to which culture played second fiddle. Michael, the executive director of the Samoan Community Development Center spoke up and said that he did not think that DHS should focus on culture when making these placement decisions. He said that he was tired of all this talk of culture—that he was simply interested in competent families. After Michael's speech, for the first time I saw that in the United States, families could be defined as cultural or acultural, competent or not. I had gone into this meeting expecting the DHS representative to be besieged by versions of what constituted Samoan culture and how his clients might be enacting that culture. But this did not happen. I had never expected competent families to be a more salient category than cultural families.

Michael and other Samoan community workers in San Francisco were not being the strategic cultural experts I was accustomed to after having spent so much time among similarly situated migrants in New Zealand. In New Zealand, it felt impossible to have a conversation with government representatives about families without invoking cultural differences. In San Francisco it seemed impossible to insert such differences into apparently similar dialogues.

On the surface, this was a meeting designed to strengthen alliances between city officials and community-based organizations in San Francisco. Like many other moments in my fieldwork among Samoan migrants living in New Zealand and the United States, it was also a meeting about how best to respond to neoliberal reforms conveyed through legislation designed to chart the divide between government bureaucracies and families. At the time of my fieldwork, 1996–1998, both New Zealand and the United States social welfare systems were responding to recent massive reforms of the welfare infrastructure. In New Zealand, people were still trying to adjust to the Children, Young Persons, and Their Families Act (1989), which had made families more responsible in deciding how to respond to cases of child abuse or juvenile delinquency. Meanwhile in the United States, people were facing the first two-year deadline for ending welfare support created by the 1996 Personal Responsibility and Work Opportunity Reconciliation Act. Governments everywhere were beginning to reimagine their relationships and obligations to families under neoliberalism. While people were responding to neoliberal legislative reforms in both my field sites, their responses in New Zealand were markedly different than their responses in the United States. The distinct analytical categories they used to do so—in particular, how and when differences were made cultural—affected how people responded in practice to various government interventions.

This was a meeting that was possible only because of the historical trajectories of globalization and colonialism. Each person at the table had complicated histories replete with the forms of hybridity enabled by the infrastructures also creating globalization. For example, the multiple ways in which these migrants engage with Christianity were embodied in the meeting. One of the Samoan organizations, Soul'd Out Productions, was a new evangelical Christian organization formed to help Samoan youth lead a more Christian life. Alofa, another Samoan organization representative, was a Jehovah's Witness, belonging to a multicultural church and to an older wave of reforming Christian movements. A third community organizer was part of a church that had been established by John Williams, the first London Missionary Society missionary to Samoa. And there were more historical traces of globalization present in the room. Alofa was intermarried and thus found that in her family, people often raised the issue of when differences might be most usefully understood as cultural. Michael came from a family tradition of navigating U.S. government bureaucracies and national borders; his father was a customs official in American Samoa.

Every person at the meeting, including me, was consciously experimenting with different categories for talking about these instances of globalization. The discussion I sparked was familiar for everyone there: people
were sometimes invoking culture and at other times invoking explicitly
acultural categories for thinking about families and communities. No one
was in accord about how and when to use culture as an analytical category
to frame certain interactions. In fact, throughout my year of fieldwork in
California, Michael was constantly trying to figure out new ways to forge
alliances with other groups, alliances that did not have cultural difference
at the core. I witnessed many other moments when he would refuse to
use culture as a conceptual frame for social relationships, much to the dis-
may of others in his organization. People often found culture useful to
think with, but not always, and not always when others were finding culture useful. And they were equally concerned with what they counted to
varying degrees as acultural—the "competent" families, capitalism, some
forms of Christianity, and so on.

In this second half of the book I examine Samoan migrants' engagements with U.S. and New Zealand government bureaucracies, exploring
how Samoan migrants and government officials produce cultural differences together. In the previous chapters, I have discussed how Samoan
migrants manage hybrid contexts within Samoan families and Samoan
communities—contexts in which capitalism and ritual exchange or different forms of Christianity are simultaneously present and need to be kept
distinct. I described some techniques Samoan migrants will use within their
own communities to demarcate cultural differences. In the next chapters,
I turn to Samoan migrants' experiences with government bureaucracies
historically shaped by encounters with other, more dominant minorities.
Because of how government bureaucracies function in both countries, I
focused during fieldwork on those people who have the fraught role of
being a cultural expert, speaking on behalf of Samoan communities in bureaucratic contexts.

People's reflexive understandings remain a central issue. Yet the questions surrounding reflexivity are different in the next three chapters. Up
until now, I have been discussing how Samoan migrants continually rees-
tablish the boundaries between social orders, and how they might move
between these social orders. In the next three chapters, I discuss a clash
of reflexivities, in which Samoan migrants are confronted with the ways

in which U.S. and New Zealand government officials understand social orders should operate.[1] In the remaining chapters, contexts become hybrid for reasons other than in the first part. For the rest of the book, I explore how people with very different ideas of what it means to belong to and reproduce a social order interact with one another. In the next three chapters, people on the ground were constantly trying to determine when and how to invoke culture when faced with people with different assumptions about culture, a dilemma sparked in part because of both New Zealand and U.S. governments' focus on multiculturalism in the wake of civil rights movements.

Governments' Multiculturalisms

Since the 1970s, liberal governments have been struggling with the question of how best to govern a heterogeneous population (Benhabib 2002; Fleras and Elliot 1992; Greenhouse 1998; Povinelli 2002). In doing so, governments are responding to migrant group's different historical trajectories. Historically some differences become more significant than others when dominant and politically vocal minorities and government bureaucracies negotiate how governments could best respond to a population's varied needs (Williams 1989). Each government thus has its own historically and dialogically constituted understandings of what counts as the relevant difference that then serves as the basis for policies. When the New Zealand government legislates for a diverse population, this legislation is shaped by their long-standing historical debates with Māori and indigenous right claims. In the United States, the policies emerge in the historical context of slavery, mistreatment of indigenous populations, and the trajectories of various migrant groups.

---

1. Here I am using *reflexivity* in a sense that owes far more to a linguistic anthropological approach, as laid out by John Lucy (1999), than it does to accounts of ethnographic reflexivity that might seen more familiar to anthropological readers (see Boyer in press for an insightful history of the structural conditions underlying anthropologists' own use of reflexivity in their writing). A linguistic anthropological sense of reflexivity stresses how an awareness of the contextually specific ways in which self, agency, and others are interrelated through language and practice. From this perspective, reflexivity is contextually bound and specific to the assumptions about social order at play in that particular content.

This has affected who becomes the major minorities and who becomes the minor minorities in both countries. The debates in New Zealand about biculturalism and multiculturalism are largely dominated by the historical relations between the government and New Zealand's major minority, Māori (see Hill 2010). In the United States, parallel debates about multiculturalism have emerged out of long-standing interactions between the government and major minorities such as African Americans, Hispanics, and Asian Americans. When minor minorities, such as Samoan migrants, encounter implemented New Zealand or U.S. multicultural policies, they are encountering definitions of difference constituted by these long-standing engagements between governments and dominant minorities. As I discussed in part I, Samoans also have their own definitions of what counts as significant cultural difference and believe that there are appropriate ways to deploy these differences strategically in political contexts. As a result, some government definitions of difference are more useful and usable for Samoans than others. One theme for the second half of the book is why definitions of culture generated by long-standing Māori–government interactions might be more conducive for Samoan migrants than definitions of difference in U.S. government dialogues with dominant minorities.

Scholars of migration have been using their comparative impulses to reveal how government policies have been affecting different minority groups' experiences (Brodkin 1998; Dusenbery 1997; Foner 2005; Loury, Madood, and Teles 2005; Shukla 2003). In particular, Verne Dusenbery and Nancy Foner have trained their comparative gazes on different governments' efforts to shape an ethnoscape, exploring how a minority group—Sikhs or Jamaicans, respectively—has one set of opportunities in one country, and a different set in another (Dusenbery 1997; Foner 2005). These scholars have applied Brackette Williams's (1989) insight that nation-states create unequal hierarchies of ethnicities to reveal how government policies affect interethnic relationships. They point out that migrants' relative successes are orchestrated by government policies because governments construct histories of inequalities through their migration policies as well as by applying social services unevenly.

Both Foner and Dusenbery delineate the hazards of treating some minority communities as members of larger categories—Jamaicans as African Americans or Sikhs as Asian Canadians. In each case, the groups lose out as a result of these governmentally imposed alliances. How do government policies forged over time in response to the political needs of major minorities affect the minor minorities who endeavor to navigate the same ethnoscape? This is precisely the question Samoan migrants in New Zealand and the United States face as they navigate an ethnic hierarchy shaped by government policies geared toward other minority groups.

In both New Zealand and the United States, Samoan migrants are minor minorities in an ethnic constellation dominated by dominant or major minority groups. In New Zealand, Samoan migrants have moved to a country where indigenous Māori grievances frame national debates. Because Māori are Polynesians, the government has historically linked immigrant Pasifika people with Māori when addressing their socioeconomic problems. In New Zealand, both Māori and Samoans are understood to be culture-bearers along similar lines. As a consequence, when the government decides that Māori culture should be supported through various grant opportunities and government programs, Samoan migrants eventually benefit as well. In sharp contrast, Samoan migrants in the United States are located primarily through census categories instead of shared cultural backgrounds. Samoan migrants were defined as "other" until the 1980 U.S. census, when Samoans were placed in a fundable ethnic category: Asian/Pacific Islander. As a result, during my fieldwork, Samoans were able to receive government services as Asian/Pacific Islanders. Yet Asian/Pacific Islander was a census category that covers too many classifiably distinct cultural groups, undermining most attempts to fashion a single migrant culture as a fundable one in the U.S. context (Hing 1993; Omi 1999). Since 2000, Samoans have been classified alongside Native Hawaiians, shifting their access to government resources yet again.

During the time that people from Samoa have been migrating to New Zealand there has been a substantial shift in the ways in which the New Zealand government imagines its obligations and commitments to Māori and, as a consequence, to other minorities as well. In response to long-standing Māori activism, from the late 1970s on government agencies began to reevaluate how they delivered services to Māori, changing their policies and practices from focusing on the individual/state relationship to emphasizing the community/state connection. While there have been many economic, social, and political factors that have contributed to this sea change, the Treaty of Waitangi has become the highly charged icon through which New Zealanders discuss these transformations. When the Treaty of Waitangi was signed in 1840, it allocated different forms of sovereignty to the British Crown and the five hundred Māori chiefs signing. Ever since, the precise meaning of the Treaty of Waitangi has been a topic of controversy (Orange 1987). However, over the last three decades, both Māori and the New Zealand government have reached a tentative consensus that the Treaty granted legal authority to the Crown while allowing Māori to retain control over resources, including cultural ones.

Most important, both Māori and the New Zealand government now agree that the Treaty of Waitangi guaranteed that the government would protect Māori culture, which it failed to do during many years of assimilationist policies. The New Zealand government began to acknowledge that the Treaty protected Māori culture as well when the Privy Council in 1994 recognized that Māori language was a *taonga*—a treasure that the Crown had promised to protect under the Treaty. In an attempt at restitution, the New Zealand government has begun supporting Māori culture in numerous ways, including supporting traditional units of social organization, such as *iwi* (which often means tribe or clan). The New Zealand government's commitment to making restitutions for Treaty violations has included increasingly allowing Māori to determine how services should best be delivered to their communities. This change is the result of a long-standing battle, in which the New Zealand government now acknowledges that, in the past, it had frequently undercut the way in which communities managed their own resources.

How to Have Fundable Samoan Culture in New Zealand

The emphasis on the Treaty of Waitangi has impacted Samoan migrants in several significant ways. First, Māori have been effectively divorced from immigrant Pasifika people, both bureaucratically and in the public imagination. Māori are now occupying a unique ethnic space in New Zealand, as the indigenous people that the postcolonial state has failed. Other ethnic minorities are largely excluded from this debate about minority identity in New Zealand (see Bozic-Vrbancic 2003; Goldsmith 2003). This exclusion was not something that Samoans working in the New Zealand government would mention resenting. In my interviews, Pacific Island policy analysts invariably told me that they were content to have Māori injustices addressed first by the government. They felt strongly that the Māori grievances had priority. Richard Hill comments on how this position was widespread: "many Pasifika (and other immigrant) leaders accepted the logic of Tangata Whenua [people of the land] demands that bicultural policies be put in place before the needs and wants of other elements of society were addressed, at least in structural ways" (Hill 2010, 305–306).

As many scholars have pointed out, by focusing on the Treaty contract, Māori have successfully made biculturalism the central framework for discussing how the government should administer to a diverse population (Fleras and Spoonley 1999; Goldsmith 2003; Pearson 1990). Māori culture has become a template for defining what counts as significant cultural difference. Pasifika people now invoke practices that Māori use to construct cultural differences when arguing for their uniqueness. They will stress how culturally unique, and thus implicitly culturally distinct from Māori, they are in their rites of passage, funerals, forms of leadership and communities, language, or extended families.

In the past two decades, Pasifika people have begun to benefit from the complex negotiations between Māori advocates and New Zealand government officials as they attempt to forge a bicultural nation-state.[2] Once the Māori successfully established government's obligations to fund education, television stations, and job training, Samoans, too, have been able to receive funds for university scholarships, language nests (language-immersion preschools), and television shows. A typical example is the Department of Social Welfare's commitment to a policy document called "Pate Lali Nafa: Strategy for Pacific Islands Employment and Service Delivery."[3] This Department of Social Welfare's policy statement was directly inspired by an earlier document geared toward Māori social workers—"Puao-te-Ata-tu: The 1986 Report of a Ministerial Advisory Committee on a Māori Perspective for the Department of Social Welfare." Like its Māori equivalent, the

---

2. Pasifika activists were also working alongside Māori activists to change government policies (see Hill 2010).

3. *Pate, lali,* and *nafa* all refer to wooden gongs in Samoan. The smallest, the *pate,* is originally thought to be from Tahiti or the Cook Islands; Tongans introduced the *lali;* and the *nafa* is thought to be originally Samoan (Buck [Te Rangi Hīroa] 1930, 576–578).

document provides guidelines for how the Department of Social Welfare should treat its Pacific Island employees and clients. Now staff can wear formal Pacific Island dress, visit traditional healers during work hours, and take longer and more flexible bereavement leaves. The staff at the Department of Social Welfare is encouraged to recognize fellow workers as culturally different, an awareness that the Department hoped would extend to their clients in beneficial ways. Once the Department of Social Welfare committed itself to supporting Māori culture, Pasifika people were able to insist that they be granted similar prerogatives.

For Samoan migrants in New Zealand, the cultural valence attached to bureaucratically constructed ethnicity has been a double-edged sword. Until Treaty claims dominated the national imagination, the government tended to use a homogenizing vision of Polynesian culture that lumped together Māori and all Pasifika people. This served to obscure significant differences among groups in their legal status as well as in their access to educational and financial resources (see Teaiwa and Mallon 2005, 208–210). This erroneous conflation generated ethnic hierarchies by forcing Māori and Pasifika people to compete with each other for limited resources on an uneven playing field. In attempts to redress historical injustices, the New Zealand government has started fostering attempts to preserve and strengthen minority groups' culture. This move goes hand in hand with the New Zealand government's neoliberal policies, which strongly urge the privatization of government services. In this case, the Māori and Samoan communities sometimes feel that they are benefiting from this decentralization. The government's commitment to supporting culture to some degree has entailed recognizing that these minority communities have their own structures of authority and ways of managing resources. As a result, currently in New Zealand, ideally (never in practice) every community has equal access to resources, which are then distributed internally in culturally appropriate ways. While Samoan migrants are often limited in political arenas to championing their own hierarchies (chiefly or church based) when seeking to address inequalities, they are able to use strategies they have honed within their own communities successfully to do so.

Samoan migrants in New Zealand have benefited from the ways culture has been defined in New Zealand. This definition has largely been the result of historic debates and compromises between Māori and government officials. When the New Zealand government began to recognize Māori culture as a treasure protected under Treaty claims, invested Māori began the difficult task of explaining Māori culture in explicit enough terms to warrant allocating government resources. Samoan migrants have many arenas in their daily lives in which they discuss Samoan culture in ways that resonate well with more explicit accounts of Māori culture. Samoan migrants in general have little difficulty describing their culture as distinctive and as fundable as Māori culture. This has, in turn, produced economic and education opportunities in New Zealand for Samoan migrants that are absent in the United States.

Fundable Classifications in the United States

People from American Samoa began to migrate in large numbers to the United States in the 1950s,[4] just as people from independent Samoa began migrating to New Zealand. Many of the first Samoan migrants to the United States were in the U.S. military and were transferred to Hawaii or the mainland when the naval base in American Samoa was closed down in 1950. Soon their wives and relatives joined them, finding jobs in the dockyards, hospitals, or factories.

While Samoan migrants are a significant ethnic minority on the national level in New Zealand, this is not the case in the United States. Samoan migrants are simply too small a minority to matter, except in a handful of urban areas, such as Los Angeles, San Francisco, San Diego, Honolulu, and Seattle. On the federal level, Samoan migrants have tended to figure only in terms of the government's relationship with American Samoa. As U.S. nationals, they are able to travel easily between the United States and American Samoa. They can serve in the U.S. military but cannot vote in federal elections. Their status after migrating to the United States is often ambiguous enough to allow them to slip easily through bureaucratic cracks (for an early example, see Ablon 1971b).

On the local level on the U.S. mainland, Samoan nonprofit organizations have had to struggle with being square pegs trying to fit into helix-shaped

---

4. Kallen claims that by 1969, there were 9,000 Samoans in Hawaiʻi, and by the mid-1970s, more than 15,000 Samoans in California (1982: 54).

ethnic holes. By the early 1970s, San Francisco, Los Angeles, and Seattle all had Samoan nonprofit organizations with varying degrees of recognition and funding from the local governments. They were all shoe-string operations; it is only since the late 1990s that Samoan organizations have begun receiving enough funds to avoid a hand-to-mouth existence. In California, there are limited opportunities to gain any financial support for cultural activities. For example, the National Council of Samoan Chiefs organizes the only Samoan cultural activity specifically funded by California cities, Flag Day.[5] In the Bay Area, the Samoan organizations all focus primarily on helping Samoan youth; it is difficult to find funding for any other community work. These organizations have been relatively isolated, which was typical of many ethnic nonprofit organizations in the area during the mid-1990s.

At the time of my fieldwork, people from Samoa in the United States faced another obstacle that people from Samoa in New Zealand did not have to confront: a sharp division between the church and the state. When people from Samoa migrated to both countries, the church became the primary institution through which they fashioned a sense of community. In both independent and American Samoa, the social organization is fundamentally decentralized; each village is in charge of its surrounding land and inhabitants. While there is a general understanding that villages organize themselves into subdistricts, districts, and then islands, the villages retain the authority to make many of the economic and political decisions (Meleisea 1995, 22–23). Villages are organized so that power is divided between two different kinds of hierarchies: the chiefs and the church. Chiefs make decisions about the daily village activities, while the minister acts as a moral authority. The minister will often intervene in village matters by, for instance, preventing certain punishments from being meted out (Shore 1982).

When people from Samoa migrate, they have great difficulty reestablishing the village hierarchy and are far more successful establishing churches. In both countries, the first people who migrated were principally young adults—promising students who had won scholarships or good workers who would be likely to send money home. The chiefs stayed

---

5. Flag Day, April 17th, is an American nationalist holiday, commemorating the United States' acquisition of American Samoa.

back in the Samoan islands, wrestling with the delicate tasks of governing villages and negotiating with colonial powers. As a result, people overseas quickly founded Pacific Island churches but did not reinstate its parallel, the chiefly system, for a number of years. Even when the migrants became old enough to be chiefs, they were invariably from different villages, making it impossible to re-create the village hierarchy overseas.

While in New Zealand the government is willing to consult with ministers and fund churches as social service resources for Pasifika people, the U.S. government refused to do so prior to the administration of George W. Bush. Because of the division between church and state, government money can be used by churches only if they establish a secular organization under their umbrella. The church is so embedded within every aspect of the migrant Samoan communities that this division often thwarted community efforts. In 1998, the only Samoan church attempting to do outreach work in the schools in the Bay Area, Soul'd Out Productions, was an evangelical outfit that defined itself in opposition to the other Samoan churches. Local government distinguished between religion and governance in ways that Samoan migrants do not. One of the consequences is that government officials and Samoan grant writers would often describe Samoans as an isolated and closed community, largely because the best way to reach the community was through the churches.

In the United States, when local government representatives try to make contact with the Samoan community, they turn to the community-based organizations. During the time of my fieldwork, however, many Samoan migrants working in these organizations had not gone through the traditional Samoan channels; I knew of only two chiefs. I did not know of any who were presently active in Samoan churches. Many of the early founders of these organizations have been women, which places them in an awkward position in Samoan migrant communities that have been steadily shifting away from acknowledging women's rights to visible leadership. This places the community organizers in a vulnerable position vis-à-vis Samoan communities. Ironically, for the community organizers themselves, espousing cultural expertise has been a double-edged sword, one that gains them limited tangible authority in bureaucratic spaces and little sympathy in Samoan circles. I will discuss this in more detail in chapter 3.

As I mentioned earlier, Samoan migrants have had few opportunities to establish a political presence within government circles because, in the

United States, ethnicity has been racialized in a way counterproductive to people from Samoa. First, through U.S. census categories in place during my fieldwork ("Asian/Pacific Islander"), they have been lumped together with Asians, a group whose diversity prevents any attempts at claims to cultural uniqueness. This has subsequently changed, and as of 2000 Samoans are in a census category with native Hawaiians and other Pacific Islanders. Second, the major minorities in California were arguing that racial and linguistic discrimination are historically the primary causes for inequalities. Yet for Samoan migrants, the social services' lack of *cultural* fit has generated many of their problems. Last, in Samoan migrant communities, information and resources circulate through the churches. When local governments rely on non-church community organizations to connect with the Samoan communities, they perpetuate a sense of isolation. In conclusion, by thinking about community and class differences in terms of race, Californian local governments do not provide Samoan migrants with a political space for articulating or remedying the negative effects of migration on their lives.

In the United States, the government allocates resources to minorities in a way that encourages Samoan migrants to frame their needs as a U.S.–specific configuration of race and class. Bonnie Urciuoli (1996) points out that this configuration emerged shortly after Samoan migrants began migrating in larger numbers to the United States.

> Social policy since 1968 has been heavily influenced by arguments that hold excluded people responsible for their own exclusion, although such arguments have been around in one form or another for at least a century. Analysts like Edward Banfield (author of *The Unheavenly City*) and Charles Murray (author of *Losing Ground* and coauthor of *The Bell Curve*), who treat race and class as moral or intellectual attributes of individuals rather than as structural properties of social groups, served as advisors in the Nixon and Reagan administrations. Polarized thinking about race and class began to dominate U.S. politics and public policy not long after the peak of federal support for civil rights. (Urciuoli 1996, 52)

Race/class is a radically different frame than Samoan migrants will use to discuss their communities' distinctiveness in other contexts. When they need to discuss what it means to be Samoan in government contexts, they must learn a set of new assumptions about what counts as relevant difference.

In the United States, this is not an experience unique to Samoan migrants. Population diversity in the United States is treated as a diversity of race and class interwoven together—to the detriment of Samoan migrants who understand difference in terms of culture.

In New Zealand, Māori have strived to make aspects of cultural difference relevant to employers and government officials, who are aware that Māori express their connections to family and community through funerals, weddings, and other such rituals. And there is growing recognition that Māori have hierarchies with rules that are quite different from what a European New Zealander is accustomed to. To the extent that Samoan migrants also share these characteristics, it is relatively easy for them also to gain bureaucratic tolerance. As this has occurred, a new bureaucratic space for cultural experts has been increasingly established in New Zealand. The parallel in the United States is not being a cultural expert, but rather being a minority expert. In the United States, where none of the major minorities make an issue of culture in this way, the techniques through which Samoan migrants articulate their cultural differences fall on deaf government ears. People from Samoa are racialized in the United States partially because the ways they fashion their cultural identities have no place among others' well-established strategies for being an ethnic minority.

3

WHEN CULTURE IS NOT A SYSTEM

In 1998, the National Office of Samoan Affairs (NOSA), was evicted for not paying their rent in a timely fashion while I was volunteering with Samoan community organizations in San Francisco. This organization was established in 1976 to help migrants from independent and American Samoa. By the time I began fieldwork in 1998, the San Francisco branch office's major focus was housing a community day school designed to help Samoan high school students on the verge of dropping out. This school was an innovative program run by the San Francisco school district. Students facing expulsion were placed in special classrooms housed by various community organizations throughout the city. The scattered community day schools were all run through a central office and the school principal, Ben (who was not Samoan), oversaw the satellite schools.

During the eviction, Alofa, the head of the NOSA's San Francisco branch, tried to get assistance from Ben. The bureaucratic relationship between Alofa and Ben was ill defined—no one knew who was responsible for what at the NOSA school. Alofa was convinced that the principal, not

NOSA, had primary responsibility for the school. From a Samoan perspective, Ben was the "chief" of the school, the one who allocated resources and should resolve any school-related problems. He was in charge of the teacher and the teacher's aide at the school; he paid their salaries and could hire or fire them. But Alofa oversaw the classroom. She called the parents when the students skipped class. She was instrumental in deciding who would be the teacher and the teacher's aide. Several of the students who attended the school were under juvenile probation, and Alofa was their case manager. What Ben decided affected Alofa's work life, but he was not her boss, and had no say over what she did.

Alofa realized that if NOSA was evicted, then the school would be shut down. She was not on good terms with Ben personally; their interests often clashed. So she was not eager to ask for his help or to let him know that her organization was facing an eviction. It took her a few months before she was ready to approach him. By that time NOSA no longer needed simply money for the landlords; they urgently needed a new location. Alofa and I drove over to the school's headquarters, which consisted of a set of trailers in a large parking lot in a bustling Latino neighborhood. We sat down in front of Ben, and Alofa softly and humbly laid out the problem. She pointed out that the school system had several empty schools under their jurisdiction and asked if perhaps one could be given to NOSA. Since an empty school had already been given to NOSA's rival Samoan community organization, this did not seem like an unreasonable request. Ben was reluctant to do anything. He explained that he too was caught in the system, and he wasn't able to get anything done that he wanted.[1] He discussed in detail all the things he tried to accomplish but couldn't because of the system. Finally he told Alofa that, no, he wouldn't be able to help; the system was too overwhelming. Alofa listened to this patiently, but when we left his office, she turned to me furious: "No *matai* [chief] would ever do anything like that." When I asked her what she meant, she explained that a *matai* would have simply listened, nodded, and promised to do what he could. He would have accepted responsibility, and under no circumstances would he have mentioned how difficult his own position was.

---

1. Michael Herzfeld describes how common this is as a bureaucratic tactic in *The Social Production of Indifference* (1992, 145).

Alofa was frustrated with Ben's plea for empathy—his insistence that she accept his "no" because she understood his perspective and his own narrated limitations. Readers who have dealt with bureaucrats in other contexts may find this tactic familiar. Being asked to sympathize with the person who is rejecting one's request is a bit difficult to swallow. Ben was asking for an empathetic response that he was not ready to reciprocate. Alofa was also responding to another aspect of Ben's positioning: his reluctance to fully inhabit his role as principal, as "chief" of the school. This is antithetical to how Samoans discuss a subject's connection to a social order. From a Samoan perspective, people embody social order, they don't mediate social order. People have a finely nuanced set of Samoan role expectations for public contexts (Shore 1982). In Samoan contexts people will interpret and anticipate each other's behavior based on each one's structural place within a context, which is determined by categories such as the hierarchical position of one's family, one's gender, age, religion, and marital status. This was markedly different from the non-Samoan bureaucrats I met during fieldwork. Those bureaucrats could spend a considerable amount of energy and time trying to separate themselves from their roles, presenting themselves as personalities compelled by a system that they personally wished to transcend. By contrast, my Samoan interlocutors had no interest in transcending the social orders with which they interacted.

To a certain degree, both Ben and Alofa were responding to shared assumptions about sociality. They both understood that people are connected in a myriad of ways, and that every social interaction contains the question: Which kinds of connections will be made visible in this moment? The crucial, and in this case insulting, difference lay in how they understand people's relationship to their roles. The conflict lay in the different ways in which both Ben and Alofa thought it possible to be reflexive about one's connection to a larger social order. Ben portrayed his role as creating a barrier, a limitation on how he and Alofa can connect. To embody his role fully would be to sever connections with Alofa, to speak only the "no" of the system. Ben can reveal his other ways of connecting with Alofa beyond his official role only by displaying the ways in which they are both constrained, both limited and only partially committed to a system that hinders. Alofa, however, construed the matter very differently. For her, disenchantment with roles and systems does not forge commonalities. Rather, potential unity lies in how well one embodies one's role—the shared order that roles contain is the basis for sociality.

This is the story of a commonplace clash, but a clash of what? This is *not* the now familiar anthropological story of a clash of worldviews, where meanings and frameworks collide. This is not a tale about how people from one culture interact with people from another culture. My Samoan interlocutors were cosmopolitan and familiar with operating within non-Samoan frameworks. Although two different understandings of how one is agentive in a system were at stake, this is not a story of misunderstandings or translations waiting to happen. Ben, Alofa, and other people I met during fieldwork were versatile in many different contexts. Neither the migrants nor the government officials I spoke with were operating solely within one framework. There is no single culture serving as a unifying backdrop for either actor. Ben had moved to the United States from the Philippines when he was a child and still was immersed in transnational family connections. Alofa had years of experience in NOSA, was married to a man from Louisiana who claimed to be descended from Africans and native Americans among others, and went to a non-Samoan church. This is not to say she is any less Samoan, but to see her as operating only in terms of what an idealized Samoan would know does not do justice to her complex cultural expertise.

If this was not a clash of cultures, then what kind of clash was it? I would like to argue that it was a clash of reflexivities—a collision between someone who regarded himself as connected to a system and someone who saw herself as engaged with a culture, in particular, Samoan culture. This kind of clash happens frequently, especially in the intersection between government bureaucracies and migrant families. In these situations, bureaucrats often require that community representatives or family members stand for and translate their cultural order. To serve in this capacity, however, requires that they reframe the culture they represent to make it fit the parameters of the bureaucrat's system. As a consequence, Samoan community workers often find themselves negotiating spaces constructed as intersections—between cultures or between systems.

When Samoan clients or community workers enter government contexts, they are often figured as culture-bearers, in contrast to that government institution's employees, who are figured as system-carriers. Culture-bearers often face strains or limitations because they alone are marked as "having culture" in these contexts (Briggs 2001; Santiago-Irizarry 2001). This difference, between being a culture-bearer or a system-carrier, contributes to the inequalities and miscommunications that often accompany these encounters since participants understand themselves to be connected to different, perhaps incompatible forms of social orders. These can be social orders that encourage people to deploy distinctive and often clashing social strategies.

The difference between being a system-carrier and a culture-bearer is a difference in reflexivities; that is, the ways in which people understand their own possibilities and restrictions in relation to what they conceptualize as a social order. To explore the price people pay for being culture-bearers in "spaces of no culture" (Taylor 2003), in this chapter I turn to how Samoan migrants navigate government bureaucracies. I focus on the price paid when U.S. government agencies required that someone act as a Samoan cultural broker, translating knowledge between system-carriers and culture-bearers in a way that is inappropriate from a Samoan cultural perspective.

Two different forms of reflexivity are at stake in this intersection between government officials/system-carriers and Samoan culture-bearers (be they Samoan family members or Samoan community organizers). First is the reflexivity already mentioned—the ways in which people view themselves as social strategists engaged with a social order that both enables and limits their efficacy. My Samoan interlocutors would describe operating within a Samoan context as though Samoan culture was a social order with role-specific hierarchies and with roles clearly compartmentalized. They, however, never described their cultural orders as systems. Government bureaucrats would describe bureaucracy similarly; they too saw themselves as belonging to a system that was composed of clearly compartmentalized roles. Yet they would not describe bureaucracy as cultural and, indeed, often seemed to view bureaucracy as acultural.

A second, interrelated form of reflexivity comes into play as well, involving how one construes others as social strategists. In the moments when system-carriers and culture-bearers interact, not only are people explicit about their relationships to a social order, be it culture or system, but they also openly acknowledge that the other person is engaged with a different social order. Samoan migrants know that bureaucrats have a system. And in turn, government bureaucrats know when they are dealing with a Samoan family or a Samoan community organization that Samoans have culture.

One of the dilemmas in these situations is that government bureaucrats presuppose that having a culture means being able to be a cultural broker or translator. Yet from a Samoan perspective, as I will discuss, being a culture-bearer is antithetical to being a translator. The conundrums the Samoan community workers encounter in these spaces reveal conflicting assumptions about how one can relate to social orders—as Samoan culture or as a bureaucratic system. Alofa was caught between incompatible alternative ways of acting as a social strategist in a context where one's relationship *to* a social order determines how one is strategic. Alofa had a different set of possible strategies if she represented culture from a Samoan perspective versus if she was representing culture from a bureaucratic perspective.

System-Carriers versus Culture-Bearers

As I mentioned in the introduction, Samoans have been describing themselves as having had a culture long before contact with Europeans, one that they readily describe as rule governed and replete with listable values. Since both Samoan migrants and the bureaucrats they encounter are willing to treat Samoan culture as bounded and predictive of behavior, one might expect the interactions between these culture-bearers and system-carriers to go smoothly. Readers familiar with the history of Samoan colonialism might be as surprised as I was that I kept encountering failures instead of successes as my interlocutors tried to navigate U.S. government bureaucracies. After all, the history of Samoan colonialism is full of accounts in which colonial indirect rule enabled Samoan *matai* to invoke cleverly and effectively reified notions of Samoan culture for their district, village or family's benefit (see Meleisea 1987a, 1987b). Even my earlier fieldwork in New Zealand among Samoan migrants led me to believe that mutually agreeing to essentialize Samoan culture could be to Samoan migrants' benefit. Yet despite my interlocutor's comfort at being culture-bearers, they still faced many problems with the ways in which U.S. government bureaucracies required them to represent Samoan culture, especially when the bureaucracies expected them to act as cultural brokers.

I conducted fieldwork with Samoan migrants after scholars, inspired by anthropology's reflexive turn, became prolifically concerned with how anthropologists use culture (Abu-Lughod 1991; Brightman 1995; Gupta and Ferguson 1992; Wagner 1981; Yengoyan 1986). As a result, I had grown suspicious of my own inclinations to bear witness for Samoan culture, and I have tried to avoid doing this throughout this book. The people I met while doing fieldwork had no such reservations. They readily depicted the social orders they understood themselves to be engaged with as cultures or systems, and they rarely confused one with the other. Although terms such as "culture" and "system" are often analytical terms used exclusively by the anthropologist, in my fieldwork and in this chapter, this is not the case. All my interlocutors used the terms "culture" and "system" to describe social orders people engaged with. Those who discussed belonging to a system never described the system as cultural, and those who talked about belonging to a culture never described the culture as a system. For my interlocutors in the field, these were two distinct forms of social orders, and each form of social order empowered at the same time as it limited the strategists involved. In this chapter, *social order* will be the general term, with *culture* and *system* deployed as ethnographically nuanced terms specific to Samoan culture and government bureaucratic systems.

My interlocutors described how one can be a social strategist relating to a social order, defined either as culture or as system. This is what I have been calling a reflexive stance. *Reflexivity*—seeing oneself as a social strategist both limited and empowered by the structures of a social order—is my term; culture and system are my interlocutors'. An important way in which Samoan culture as a social order differed from a government system is in the kind of movements, or translations, between social orders that each tacitly allowed. For reasons I will discuss later in this chapter, Samoans did not believe that people could move easily across multiple social orders, while those engaging with a government system did. Thus people had strikingly different beliefs about whether translation was possible, depending on what they understood about how people can engage with social orders. Translation is thus a social strategy that depends on the kinds of agency people on the ground believed realizable. Whether or not translation was socially possible is a question of reflexivity.

Reflexivity in a Samoan Perspective

In the intersection between government systems and cultural families, the government bureaucracy often will rely heavily on two sorts of cultural mediators to navigate these intersections—representatives and translators. *Representatives* are mediators who are expected to speak for the interests of their communities. This type of mediator is one that Samoan migrants often can easily produce. The second type of mediator that government systems require is a cultural *translator*—those who are expected to solve problems created by the disjunctures between bureaucratic efforts to regulate families and the ways in which people are living their lives. These mediators are often community workers who are expected to translate both language and culture in order to resolve the problems that government bureaucracies have framed as cultural misunderstandings.

Governments require these two forms of cultural mediators to promote a specific form of multiculturalism. This multicultural governance hinges on supporting and interacting with ethnic communities as entities with unified needs and agendas. Not surprisingly, when bureaucracies define differences as cultural, cultural mediators are seen as conduits for circumventing the cultural misunderstandings possible in any cross-cultural interaction. Manuals and articles on how to be a cultural broker have sprung up (e.g., Gregory 1993; Jezewski 1995; National Center for Cultural Competence 2004), providing instructions on how best to mediate between cultures and systems. So as governments increasingly invoke multiculturalism as a lens through which to understand populations, cultural brokers become more and more fashionable from schools' or welfare services' perspectives. Yet Samoans are often ambivalent about this type of translator and frequently do not trust them enough to allow them to occupy their governmentally assigned role.

What do the two kinds of cultural mediators that multicultural governments require look like from a Samoan perspective? There are aspects of both representatives and translators that resonate strongly with the ways in which my interlocutors would discuss cultural agency. While being a cultural mediator is an act of translation, it is also always an act of representation: people are always speaking for what a culture is meant to be at the same time as they are recontextualizing cultural knowledge. From a Samoan perspective, it is this act of representation that is most salient and achievable. Every Samoan extended family has at least one *matai,* a person who speaks for and about the family's interests in political contexts. It is this long-standing tradition of such representation that has led people in Samoa to declare that they were "democratic" (in the form of political representation) for centuries before colonialism (see Tcherkézoff 1998).

Yet Samoan *matai* are not Samoan social workers. Thus the question becomes how and when do the forms of representation that Samoans regularly practice become relevant in their encounters with government bureaucracy. To address such representation—and by this I mean representation with a political edge, or how people stand for and speak for others in a Samoan context—I turn to what it means to be a *matai* in Samoan communities. Every *matai* speaks for his or her family's or group's interests in different contexts, such as village council meetings and in ritual exchanges such as weddings and funerals. Chiefly titles are not inherited through primogeniture: when a title becomes available, the elders of the family hold several meetings and decide who should be the next title-holder. There are two kinds of chiefs: high chiefs (*ali'i*) and talking chiefs (*tulafale*). Every high chief has a talking chief who speaks for the joint title in ritual encounters. These two kinds of chiefs express power in distinct ways. The *high chief* is the decision maker, the arbitrator, the one who weaves together the differing political positions that people take into a unified stance that the family or the village adopts. The high chief embodies the moments in which group relations can become unified wholes. The *talking chief* is, conversely, the boundary maker (Tcherkézoff 1993). He or she is the active one, the one who discusses people's genealogical connections, making visible the interconnections that link all those present at a ceremonial meeting (which always also entails disregarding other possible connections). The talking chief performs the tasks in Samoan contexts that are most analogous to the tasks required by cultural mediators who represent. In addition to delineating genealogical paths, talking chiefs also publicly invoke the signals that are commonly understood to mark tradition—metaphors, mythical allusions.[2]

I have been describing chiefs as representatives of extended families and political actors in village contexts largely because Samoan social

---

2. For fuller accounts of Samoan chieftainship, see Duranti 1994; Shore 1982; and Tcherkézoff 1993, 1998, 2000.

organization historically has been decentralized. Being able to represent or stand for a village, subdistrict, district, or island has been a highly contested achievement. The hierarchy among chiefs is most clearly delineated within villages, and when comparing chiefs from different islands or different districts it is often difficult to evaluate which title is more prestigious. Most chiefly titles do not belong to a centralized hierarchy; their relative status can be determined only adequately on a village level. While conceptually it should be possible to compare titles, in practice this would be too politically fraught to be tenable.

Migrating created a new twist in this tension between village practice and cultural ideals. When people migrated, they joined neighborhoods with people who originally belonged to many different Samoan villages. When they began to form new churches, this immediately became a problem. In Samoa, the village church hierarchy and the village chiefly hierarchy are symbiotically intertwined but in practice serve as sources for different forms of power. While the minister provides spiritual leadership for the village, he is not supposed to be intimately involved in governing the village. The national church administration places the minister in the village after seminary training and, ideally, has chosen a village where the minister has no relatives. He cannot hold a title and is not expected to help decide the village's daily functioning. Church positions, such as deacons, treasurer, and secretary, will be held by *matai,* but this tends not to generate most of the struggles for power. This separation was impossible to preserve in migration, where no village hierarchy is present to serve as a blueprint for various church roles.

Because the Samoan churches in diaspora have, out of necessity, members from different villages, congregants cannot determine status by comparing chiefly titles. Within overseas churches, people got into bitter conflicts when they tried to determine the status of various titles on an intervillage level. For those involved, it would be insulting to attribute a higher status to a title from another village. Consequently, migrants were not able to re-create village hierarchies overseas successfully. A minister in Wellington explained to me that this was one of the most positive outcomes of migrating to New Zealand. He said that in New Zealand, every *matai* was equal—no one was greater than any one else. From his perspective, migration had formed a more harmonious space, without many of the conflicts that shifting hierarchies fostered in Samoa.

But this new equality also left Samoan communities in a bind when they have to have representatives speak in government contexts. Speaking for Samoan interests in diasporic contexts is a privileged and contentious position. People are often loath to credit another chiefly title with the privilege to speak for Samoan communities in general. This too undercuts their own families' pride, or their villages' pride, or their islands' pride. There are no traditional routes through which people can fashion themselves representatives of Samoan migrant communities in political arenas. People are assigned this role by the New Zealand or U.S. government, not necessarily by their local Samoan communities. So, despite the fact that Samoan *matai* might seem like a ready-made cultural representative to speak for Samoan interests in bureaucratic contexts, this is not easily accomplished in diaspora. Samoan representatives are rarely chosen by the city's churches or chiefs; this position is a job that one is hired to do or volunteers to do following government expectations, not Samoan ones. Often there are no established paths toward becoming a representative endorsed by all the Samoan communities of an area. Despite various attempts over the years, there is no Samoan chief for Los Angeles, San Francisco, or Seattle—the chiefly system does not reiterate itself along spatial lines when outside of Samoa. Outside of independent and American Samoa, standing for Samoan communities has become a contentious and readily undermined achievement.

While migrant communities might accept people who attempt to represent Samoan culture in government settings, albeit with reservations, they tend to be far more reluctant to engage with people positioned as cultural translators. U.S. government agencies have relied on cultural translators to assist members of Samoan communities since the mid-1960s (Joan Ablon, personal communication). These cultural translators are often younger people who have had institutional training in negotiating non-Samoan contexts: social workers, lawyers, and so on. These brokers are not always well-respected in their communities. From a Samoan perspective, translators are contentious figures and their assistance is often rejected. Representatives of other Asian/Pacific Island communities in the Bay Area, such as Cambodian, Vietnamese, Chinese, or Korean, did not seem to face similar rebuffs from their clients. This rejection is partially a result of how one understands relationships to cultural knowledge as a Samoan. From a Samoan perspective, Samoan cultural brokers are often seen as violating cultural imperatives and as being willing to act against their own communities' interests. Yet U.S. government agencies presuppose that cultural mediation is an essential tool toward promoting cultural diversity, rewarding some people with multiple cultural fluencies who are expected to act as skillful cultural translators.

Translation is, as I have mentioned earlier, the most difficult aspect of being a cultural broker from a Samoan perspective to accept. Here I am not talking about the linguistic act of translation; people move between languages frequently. But translation is not only about linguistic meanings. As Walter Benjamin points out in "The Task of the Translator," "Translatability is an essential quality of certain works, which is not to say that it is essential that they be translated; it means rather a specific significance inherent in the original manifests itself in its translatability" (Benjamin 1968, 71). Benjamin urges a focus on translatability as a quality that a work or idea can possess, transforming the ways in which one thinks of translation as a process. He moves away from a form–content dichotomy, arguing that it is neither form nor content whose distinctiveness sabotages translation. Instead, translatability in Benjamin's account is dependent on the ways in which the text is intertextual in the broadest sense, the degree to which the meaning of a statement is derived from the interwoven texture of a language's words (Benjamin 1968, 78). Translation thus is not derived from a one-to-one correspondence between words. Rather, the translator must respond to words' historical and emotional connotations, moving words from one web of meaning to another. Benjamin presents the possibility that some texts might not possess the quality of translatability, although given Benjamin's intellectual investments, this is not a possibility he explores. Benjamin's suggestion that translatability exists outside of the confines of form and content, and is a quality linked to perspective, resonates with how my Samoan interlocutors would engage with cultural knowledge. Benjamin saw all great work as translatable, whereas cultural knowledge, from a Samoan perspective, does not possess this quality of translatability.[3]

This is not to say that Samoans frame cultural knowledge as *literally* untranslatable.[4] People I encountered were willing, particularly in

---

3. See also Deborah Kapchan 2003 for a discussion of how people on the ground have beliefs about language that shape their understandings of translation.

4. Mattijs van de Port (1999) discusses how Serbians also see their own cultural knowledge as untranslatable; his term is "obstinate otherness." For van de Port, Serbians' claims

government or school contexts, to name core Samoan cultural values— both in Samoan and in English. To explain what it means to be a Samoan, people can turn to a readymade set of phrases such as *tautua* (service), *fa'aaloalo* (respect), *alofa* (compassion and love), *ava* (reverence), and so on. As I mentioned earlier, these are the terms that people representing Samoanness easily produced in the context of government training sessions when asked what Samoan cultural values were (and for which they would readily offer English translations). Both bureaucratic system-carriers and Samoan culture-bearers are willing to define culture in terms of values. The difference lies in how each relates to values. The government officials will describe a person's role as an instrumental means toward achieving a value. From a Samoan perspective, roles embody values— inhabiting a role is the same as practicing or being a value. One of the consequences of this perspective is that values are fundamentally not translatable for people engaged in being Samoan because a value can exist only within a particular situation and performance, not abstracted from the situation. Listing Samoan cultural values in training workshops is a far cry from understanding or conveying Samoan cultural knowledge. Ideological assertions of what constitutes Samoan culture are not, from a Samoan perspective, effective translations of Samoan culture into other registers. Samoanness lies not in explicit reformulations but in appropriate contextual behavior that reveals a sophisticated cultural knowledge of how the context itself has come to be.

From a Samoan perspective, cultural knowledge is not translatable largely because it is presumed to always be situated knowledge. As I mentioned, translating presumes that the cultural knowledge and cultural roles can be disentangled from their contexts, and thus denying the context. When I started asking why Samoan community workers seemed out of favor with local Samoan communities, my interlocutors would explain that Samoans didn't trust community workers; the workers were perceived as embezzling government money. Yet other figures in Samoan communities were invariably described as corrupt as well. Church ministers and chiefs were constantly being described as embezzling large sums of money. I heard many rumors of ministers in New Zealand and the United States

---

of incommensurability result not from language ideology but as a response to experiences of violence.

who embezzled from their congregation until they were kicked out. They left for Samoa, began a church there, and when they were kicked out for embezzling in Samoa, they started a church again in the city where they first began. They were always able to start churches anew. When people told me these rumors, they expressed disbelief and frustration at how willing other Samoans were to accept and respect ministers, regardless of previous failings. Some rumors of corruption seemed more effective than others at preventing people from doing their job. The crucial difference between Samoan ministers and Samoan social workers seems to be that Samoan ministers are operating wholly within contexts shaped by Samoan expectations. Samoan ministers had clear-cut roles in Samoan contexts, roles that contained intelligible expectations, in which the mediation was between God and the community rather than the community and a non-Samoan government. In short, representing is acceptable from a Samoan perspective, while translating is not.

Various ethnographers of Samoa have argued that the fluidity of social roles is contextually determined rather than determined by set attributes. People act like respectful and subservient daughters-in-law because of the context, not because those qualities are part of their internal personality (Mageo 1998; Shore 1982). One cannot choose one's role, although one can have some control over which roles are thrust upon oneself. The reflexivity called for by a Samoan context is the awareness of how best to embody one's role fully, to understand the ramifications of everyone's role in a given context, and to make visible the aspects of the role that are most strategically advantageous. To successfully negotiate a given situation is often also to encourage others to adopt the role that one might find most profitable for that particular encounter. Inasmuch as Samoan roles serve as a bundle of guidelines for the types of obligations and respect two people owe each other, it is important for people to be able to predict how a context will be interpreted to ensure that others adopt the most circumstantially useful role.

Other scholars of Pacific diasporas have commented on how contextually specific Pacific migrants' identity claims are (McGrath 2003; Spickard 2002; Tupuola 2003). These authors all focus on how people's identities shift depending on the context—people will claim to be Hawaiian, Samoan, or Māori in different situations. Spickard writes: "In the first place, Pacific Islander American ethnicity seems to be *situational*. Dorri Nautu has

Hawaiian, Filipino, Portuguese, and several other ancestries. She lives in a mixed community of part-Hawaiians, Hawaiians, and several other ethnic groups, and she is qualified to attend the university on an ethnic Hawaiian scholarship. She identifies herself more than anything else as Hawaiian. But, she says, 'If I'm with my grandmother, I'm Portuguese. If I'm with some of my aunts on my dad's side, I'm Filipino. If I'm hanging around, I'm just local. If I'm on the mainland, I'm Hawaiian'" (Spickard 2002, 44). This quote epitomizes the multiplicity of identities that scholars of Samoans have already discussed at a different level of scale. As I mentioned, both Shore (1982) and Mageo (1998) discuss how the context determines who the person is at that moment, be it a quiet and deferential daughter-in-law or a charismatic and voluble Sunday school teacher. These authors all focus on how people shift roles, personalities, and identity claims as they move between contexts. Here, I am focusing on a different aspect of this phenomenon: how important the context is for determining who people can be.

The most sophisticated cultural expertise comes from understanding the rules and interconnections so well in a given context that one can elicit the desired relationships and actions from others.[5] Given this, the Samoan perspective offers pitfalls for people who wish to cross between social orders by translating. Reframing cultural knowledge becomes troublesome, overlooking how one can possess cultural knowledge in the first place. In addition, being a cultural translator undercuts other people's abilities to strategize in a Samoan manner—to be able to shift cultures as a translator prevents others' ability to affect the role one will inhabit in a given situation. One could be acting from the vantage point of either culture at any moment. The epistemological assumptions necessary to make a person predictable or an object of strategy from a Samoan perspective are not in place when the person acts as a mediator. No wonder Samoan cultural translators are so often described as untrustworthy—the nature of

---

5. A Samoan lawyer explained to me this level of expertise when discussing how Samoans recite each others' genealogies with savvy at the beginning of any political meeting. He gave me a hypothetical situation: Imagine that one village is visiting another to gain support for their political candidate. The visiting village's orator will judiciously tweak the truth, and present the host village as connected to the head of state. The host village will be flattered and unwilling to debunk this connection. In addition, they will hopefully feel magnanimous toward the visiting village for this assertion.

the translator's role undercuts the potential for others to be strategically effective from a Samoan perspective.

The role of translator is difficult for Samoans to accept because it presumes substitution. Translators are all theoretically substitutable for each other from a bureaucratic perspective. Anyone with the necessary cultural and linguistic knowledge is acceptable as a translator. Yet from a Samoan perspective, no one is substitutable in any context.[6] Who they are, their genealogical and lived connections, help determine what the context will be. The problem is not so much that translators move between government systems and Samoan culture, but rather that the role of translator presupposes a neutral, nonembedded position within Samoan culture. This is a position that Samoan migrants do not believe can exist. Samoan community workers may seem substitutable from the point of view of government systems, but from a Samoan point of view, they are always already enmeshed within Samoan networks.

In short, while representatives are problematic from a Samoan perspective because of how Samoan hierarchies change in diaspora, translators present a paradox for epistemological reasons. When cultural mediators translate, the action presupposes that cultural knowledge has a quality of translatability, that one's relationship to cultural knowledge is portable and mutable, not fundamentally situational. Being Samoan entails representing a contextually bound role, staying within a Samoan perspective, not moving between perspectives. It is this epistemological assumption about how one should be related to cultural knowledge that makes cultural translators unpredictable from a Samoan perspective.

The Reflexivity in a System

Up until now in my analysis, government bureaucracies and their epistemological assumptions have been in the background, tacitly framing the requirements that Samoan community workers often found difficult to navigate. I want to turn to why a government bureaucracy might require that Samoan community workers be translators that their own

---

6. My thanks to Teri Silvio for pointing this out.

communities will not support. Here I rely heavily on Niklas Luhmann,[7] a systems theorist who offers an analytical account of how systems operate that I find resonates with the bureaucratic systems that government officials enacted and described in San Francisco (Luhmann 1990, 1995). I am using Luhmann in this analysis to understand the epistemological assumptions underlying bureaucrats' reflexivity, not to comprehend the bureaucrats' reality.[8] According to Luhmann, every system is autopoietic; that is, solely constituted by its own processes. He writes that systems "create everything that they use as an element and thereby use recursively the elements that are already constituted in the system" (Luhmann 1995, 444). All the components of a system, such as the forms and circulating knowledge, are coded, constituted, and reconstituted according to the system's own criteria. This ensures that all meaning-making activities, such as evaluations and analyses, can happen only within the terms defined by the particular system within which the activity occurs. Thus *reflexivity* in the context of a system is defined solely within the terms of that system; each system has its own unique set of principles that determine what counts as reflexivity or effective action. In short, it is inherent to how systems function that they define the world in their own terms, including the reflexivity embedded in that system.

While systems' solipsism ensures autonomy, systems still require input that is not defined in terms of the system. In Luhmann's terms, this is about a system's relationship with its environment: a system must have an environment that provides constant material for the system to recode and thus sustain itself. How does this abstract summary of Luhmannian systems apply to government bureaucracies? The government system requires intersections with other systems that create disorders, which then need to be resolved from within the government system. In the intersection context I am discussing, the government system's environment is principally composed of families, and in particular cultural families. So the government welfare system requires that families exist to provide the system

---

7. For a more detailed account of Niklas Luhmann's work and its relevance to ethnographers of bureaucracy, see Ilana Gershon 2005.

8. In doing so, I am shifting away from Luhmann's own premises by continually rewriting people back into an account of systems. Luhmann instead argues that people (or in his terms, "psychic systems") and social systems are distinct entities and inevitably miscommunicate.

with unorganized chunks of knowledge that must be transformed into organized information. This is the task of the bureaucrats my Samoan interlocutors encountered; the bureaucrats all were translating families into the parameters of the government system. The families often reluctantly agree to participate in this recoding in the hopes that this will assist family members in navigating other systems—the economic system or the legal system, for example.

To begin exploring ethnographically how systems might define the possibilities for reflexivity in a particular context, I turn to an encounter imbued with the explicitness common to training sessions. The setting is the San Francisco Juvenile Probation Department's first training sessions for case managers in the intensive home-based supervision (IHBS) program. This innovative program hires workers from community-based organizations to assist probation officers in monitoring youth classified as at high risk of becoming juvenile offenders. The San Francisco Juvenile Probation Department has funded the program since 1996, allocating money to community-based organizations,[9] which, in turn, hired a case worker to supervise between five and ten juveniles.[10]

Angela, the trainer, began by defining *case management*. She explained that there are three types of case management. The first involves collecting accurate information and does not entail personal interaction. She explained that most welfare officers perform this type and would not recognize a client if the officer saw them walking on the street. The second type of case management involves referral, and Angela did not elaborate. The third type of case management was what IHBS case workers were supposed to do: help transform families into functioning systems by assisting the family to articulate and meet mutually established goals.

Throughout the training session, Angela discussed how to begin treating families as systems (her term), as well as describing some difficulties the case workers might face when implementing this approach. She cautioned her audience that, as case workers, they must identify clearly who

---

9. During 1998, ten community-based organizations were involved. Only two of these organizations—the National Office of Samoan Affairs and the Vietnamese group—targeted a particular ethnic group.

10. Supervision involved calling everyday to ensure that the youth was obeying curfew, meeting with the youth three times a week, and observing the child at school once a month.

their client is as they perform certain tasks. She explained that this problem arises when one begins to view the family as a system. A case manager must constantly ask whether they are trying to assist the child, the parents, the family as a whole, or sometimes even the probation officer. Another case worker from a community-based organization, Orit, interrupted Angela and asked her if promoting the child's best interests wasn't normally also promoting the family's best interests as well. Angela was quick to explain that this is the dilemma that constantly haunts all case workers: children's interests often diverge from the family's interests as a unit. As an example, she talked about instances when judges might decide it is in the best interests of the child to be placed in foster care although this is not in the best interests of the family.

Throughout the day, Angela proceeded to outline how case workers should respond to families as systems. Here is a typical discussion from my field notes for that day:

> Angela then starts talking about strength. She says that lots of times a parent's strength and a kid's strength will work against each other. Often if you pay attention to developing or encouraging a parent or child's strength, you often end up ignoring the relationship between the two of them. Individual strength can create a tug of war, but what case managers need to do is focus on allowing the relationship to flourish.... She said that lots of times we see strengths in terms of how families fit into society, but that this is misleading. Instead, family-focused work means that we are concerned with family cohesiveness. Sometimes, when families fit well into society, it means that the parents are working so much that they don't have time to have meaningful communication with the kids. They are doing all they can to survive, but aren't putting any energy into making sure that the family functions as a unit.
>
> Orit responded by saying that she has a girl who doesn't know where or what her parents do for a living. Often her clients don't know where their siblings go to school, or how they are doing in school. There isn't even basic pooled information within the family. As she says this, other people in the room start nodding furiously–this is clearly a common phenomena.
>
> A lot of the case managers agree that families aren't communicating, that parents and kids just aren't talking at all. [Field notes, May 7, 1998]

These discussions were typical of the training sessions. Angela was suggesting that all family members relate to each other as though they are part of an integrated system, and thus are circulating information in a way similar to how an idealized welfare system circulates information. None of the case workers in training found that family members behaved as system-carriers in this sense, and most were vociferous in letting her know this. Yet Alofa, the Samoan case worker, normally was silent about how inappropriate this approach might be for Samoan families.

Alofa expressed a critique from the standpoint of a Samoan perspective only once during the six training sessions, largely because I instigated the conversation toward the end of a long training session in early June. Angela was talking about encouraging parents to meet their children's emotional needs, a perspective that I pointed out was ethnocentric because not every cultural perspective encouraged parents to see children as emotionally needy. Angela was surprised to be told that Samoans might not see their children as bearing emotional needs or requiring conversations that assessed and supported their children's emotional well being. In what I assume was an attempt to establish a common ground, Angela asked Alofa and me how Samoan parents addressed requests for lunch money or new sneakers. Alofa responded that children weren't supposed to express these needs openly. Parents were supposed to anticipate the physical needs of their children. If a child asks a parent for something, the child is implicitly criticizing the parent for failing in their parental responsibilities. In general, Alofa said, children are not seen as having needs. Instead, children have a specific role that has certain duties and obligations. Parents are also occupying their role, which entails fulfilling various responsibilities toward their children. Alofa explained that this was why most of her job as a community-based worker was teaching parenting classes—because what might be culturally appropriate in Samoa was not necessarily allowed (by the government) for Samoan families living in the United States. She described how Samoan culture often encouraged parent-child relationships that are detrimental to a child's well-being from a U.S. perspective. Despite Alofa's eloquent intervention, Angela was not persuaded. She kept insisting that to be a parent meant trying to understand and respond to one's children's needs.

After the training session, as Alofa and I chatted in the parking lot, Alofa told me that Angela's reaction was typical. When she first began going to similar training sessions, she was constantly trying to explain the Samoan perspective. She quickly realized that this was pointless, and she

now kept quiet. She told me that she had watched, amused, as I tried to intervene, and only spoke up to offer me support. In teaching case managers
how to think of families as systems, Angela was also teaching how to think
about belonging to systems, not cultures. Alofa had learned the futility of
introducing culture into this context; I had not (yet).

As I mentioned earlier, systems-carriers seem to want to sustain systems
through processes defined solely on the system's own terms. As a result,
the system-carriers must recode all input from their surroundings, such
as descriptions of how Samoan families operate, into information structured according to their own principles. Angela even refers to this coding
in her initial account of the three types of case managers. The first type,
whose sole job is to serve the welfare system, don't know their clients as
people, only as coded or codable case files. As Luhmann argues, systems
are solipsistic—requiring that all other knowledge be rearranged into information they can process.

The recoding can occur on various levels. Angela's first example of recoding, the welfare officer who wouldn't recognize a family outside the office,
is one that occurs only on the boundaries of the family—a processing that
defines how a system will refer to a family every time the system and family encounter each other. The family becomes coded as potentially changing within set parameters and with certain quantifiable features. Angela,
however, was teaching case managers to make the governmental system
fundamental to how families interact by transforming them into family systems modeled on bureaucratic systems. Luhmann points out that often the
governmental system encroaches on other systems, in this case the family
system, justifying its own existence while attempting to remake families in
its own image (1995, 213–214). This increase in administration is misplaced
because it is creating a government bureaucratic order in domains not conducive to that form of order. Not surprisingly, all the people Angela was
training protested that families simply don't process information in the way
that she was presupposing. It is telling that Orit, the first person who spoke
up to criticize Angela's approach, did so precisely by pointing to questions
of knowledge circulation. In later training sessions, Angela continued to
promote training families to behave as systems. She urged case managers
to try to help families create a plan of recovery, in which they schedule the
changes they will make each week or each month. She was presenting the
families as functional when they are self-referentially "managed" in much

the same way that government agencies are. Angela was teaching how families could be functional from a bureaucratic perspective. She was teaching case managers to replace the family's unique principles of how information and resources should circulate with bureaucratic principles, such as explicitly detailed time frames for implementing overarching plans.

In this context, culture and system become antithetical frames for understanding how families operate. They are so incompatible, in fact, that when, as described above, Alofa and I suggested moments when it would be culturally inappropriate to expect families to behave as systems, Angela responded with confusion. She told us that we were presenting Samoan families as operating according to principles that families simply do not use. In this context, and others in which the system perspective dominated, families had only a limited way to be cultural. To be cultural was to present a recodable disorder. From a system-carrier's perspective, culture wasn't a social order that explained complex hierarchical relationships or that determined how knowledge and resources might circulate. Instead, culture was an explanation for communicative failures, a frame required when people did not behave according to a system's expectations. Culture thus asserts an unstable difference, one that becomes visible only in moments requiring conflict resolution. This difference is invariably located outside of the system: the welfare system and its practitioners do not have culture, only the troublesome and unpredictable clients do. It becomes the role of cultural mediators, such as Alofa, to translate between cultural clients and system-carriers. This often becomes an impossible task because the ways in which clients relate to being Samoan does not easily mesh with how government systems operate.

Recall the encounter between Alofa and Ben, in which Alofa as cultural mediator is caught in a similar trap as Ben is vis-à-vis systems. Neither Ben nor Alofa exists wholly inside the context of the bureaucratic system and this partial commitment produces parallel constraints. Ben describes the ways he exceeds the system in terms of his personality—his wishes and personal motivations. For Alofa, it is her cultural perspective that prevents the system from subsuming her—a position created largely by her role as defined within a Samoan social order. In general, from a system's perspective, the type of agency that people can express in a system is invariably partial in the following sense. Because people are continually moving between systems in their own lives, they are often driven to be reflexive about the differences between them. In the process, they are ascribing to themselves a limited ability to manipulate systems. I am suggesting that Ben's appeal for empathy comes from his understanding of what one can actually do in a bureaucratic system. People's primary function in these bureaucratic systems is to reorder incoming information into packets that are usable and manageable by the particular system. The information always arrives in a disordered fashion, thus warranting this ordering process and compelling people to be translators. System-carriers are both translators in practice and reflexively understand their own agency as that of a translator—uneasy participants responding to systemic restrictions but never wholly immersed nor fully in control in any particular system.

When Alofa is expected to be a cultural mediator, she engages in the work of translation under special conditions. The systemic space of the state requires that she translates, while at the same time the cultural space that she is supposed to translate prohibits such acts of translation. From a Samoan perspective, when one is being cultural, one is embodying the cultural norms without any gap between self and culture. To move across this gap would be to deny fundamentally what it means to be Samoan. Community workers are suspect, largely because they are moving between two different social orders, each with its own limitations on how one can reflexively position oneself in relation to such an order. Moving reflexively between two social orders requires a relationship to cultural knowledge and to cultural roles that can be a distanced one. This relationship to knowledge and role is inimical to Samoan conceptions of culture.

How is reflexivity different when moving between cultures than when occupying a prescribed cultural space? When one moves between social orders, one is enacting the possibility of other rules or epistemological perspectives on the world. One is practicing the moral lessons taught through cultural relativism, that there is no single traditional code dictating how one should be. To be culturally versatile is to take a particular epistemological stance toward the ways in which selves can and should embody cultural knowledge—one sees cultural order as mutable. When being a culturally versatile social actor, the goal is to be able to move strategically between and across rules. In addition, this form of self-making presumes the self and the social order are fundamentally divided.[11] The aim is never to bridge the gap between self and culture, but rather to use the distance between self and culture to one's best strategic advantage. To mediate culturally is to be reflexive about one's relationship to social orders, to maneuver in the strategically fruitful gap between who one is and how one can articulate this. Yet, as I have addressed earlier, this gap between self and culture is nonsensical from a Samoan perspective. To be a cultural self from a Samoan perspective is to embody one's cultural roles as fully as possible. From a bureaucratic system's perspective, translation is both inevitable and essential; from a Samoan cultural perspective, translation moves one away from being Samoan.

As governments increasingly begin to address consciously the complexities inherent in governing a multicultural population, what counts as *culture* in multiculturalism becomes increasingly charged. Government agencies often require that those designated as "cultural" have a specific and self-conscious relationship to their cultural identity. These bureaucracies often require that culture-bearers behave according to predetermined cultural norms. In addition, certain cultural representatives will be designated as cultural mediators and expected to move easily between their communities' cultural expectations and bureaucracies' system-based expectations. This type of relationship to social orders, however, is not universally acceptable. Moving between two social orders is a task that can be accomplished from a government's perspective on cultural pluralism, but not a Samoan perspective. Mediation is contentious because the ways in which people understand their relationships to systems or cultures affects the kinds of agencies they will express. This is particularly salient in multicultural contexts, in which government officials try to govern people with potentially radically different assumptions about what it means to be part of a culture.

Samoan community workers are caught between the demands of belonging to a system and the expectations of participating effectively in Samoan cultural contexts. These impasses are largely created by *second-order reflexivities*—the understandings people have of what it means for another

---

11. This relation to social orders calls to mind a notion of performance similar to what practice theory proposes (see Bourdieu 1977; Giddens 1984).

to belong to a social order, be it a system or a culture. In encounters between members of Samoans migrant communities and government officials, the tensions revolve around the figure of the cultural broker. From a system-carrier's perspective, culture-bearers should be translators whose work is to reformulate cultural knowledge into information a system can process. From a Samoan perspective, other Samoans may not be translators of cultural knowledge but, if hierarchically appropriate, can be representatives of such knowledge. In these moments, reflexivity ironically creates not the openings between social orders but the barriers.

4

LEGISLATING FAMILIES AS CULTURAL

When I was doing fieldwork in New Zealand and in the United States from 1996 to 1998, families, community workers, and government officials all were responding to recent, transformative neoliberal legislation. In New Zealand, the Children, Young Persons, and Their Families (CYPF) Act (1989) had restructured how the New Zealand government reacted to child abuse cases and juvenile delinquency. In the United States, the welfare-to-work legislation, or Personal Responsibility and Work Opportunity Reconciliation Act (PWORA) (1996) had been passed in 1996, and everyone was concerned with the consequences of implementing the new regulations. Both pieces of legislation refashioned the intricate relationship between families and government. In the United States, the legislation realigned people's responsibility for their poverty (yet again), requiring that people be responsible for the personal effects of larger structural inequalities (see chapter 5 for a discussion of how Samoan community workers participated in a reallocation of responsibility). In New Zealand, the legislation refigured the ways people's culture played a role in how the government dealt with their family. In this chapter, I look at how legislating explicitly for culture affected Samoan migrant families in New Zealand.

The CYPF Act (1989) is the parliamentary response to critical consultations with Māori and Pacific Islanders who expressed strong reservations about the original bill. These consultations had a significant effect on the changes the Act introduced. The members of Parliament heeded the critique that the original bill was too Eurocentric and biased, and attempted to craft laws that reflected what they had been told were Māori and Pacific Island strategies for resolving family crises. In particular, the legislators introduced the Family Group Conference, which legislators believed to be based on Māori and Pacific Island techniques for resolving family conflict. Extended families, under the guidance of a social worker, met together to discuss how to best respond to child abuse or delinquent behavior. The Act was designed to encourage a range of culturally diverse family techniques for addressing child abuse and youth offenders. In doing so, the Act required families to present themselves as being cultural and redesigned many of New Zealand government techniques for dealing with families labeled at risk. In short, this legislation transformed the bureaucratic infrastructure so that it could openly accommodate cultural difference.

When I interviewed Samoan social workers about implementing this recent piece of family legislation, several responded in a way that puzzled me. They told me that Act in its raw form couldn't be brought straight to the Samoan family in its raw form. The social worker, they said, has the difficult task of raising the level of the family to the level of the Act. At the same time, social workers have to shift the way that they present the Act to their clients so that it can be more easily introduced into the Samoan family. Their descriptions confused me because they indicated that the Act was not unfolding as the stories about its origins would predict. This Act was designed to herald a new era of family policy explicitly designed to accommodate a multicultural citizenry by modeling itself on Māori and Pacific Island extended family practices. When I spoke with social workers in 1997, nine years after implementation, why were they so focused on the difficulties they faced mediating between their Samoan clients and the Act itself? The social workers were voicing the tensions caused by a mismatch of cultural expectations, yet the Act was written to circumvent precisely these problems. What created this gap between the extended families encountered by Samoan social workers and those imagined in the CYPF Act?

The words social workers used to describe bridging this gap provide clues to the nature of the gap they were encountering.[1] They did not talk to me about translating the Act into Samoan, an activity that the organizations they worked for constantly expected them to do. Rather, they discussed raising the level on which Samoan families operated and changing the level on which the Act functioned so that they could coexist on the same level. Initially I thought that they were talking about the divide between an abstract piece of legislation and the nitty-gritty realities of daily family life. When I asked one social worker if this is what he meant, he explained how the Act in its raw form could not be effectively introduced to Samoan families. With hindsight, I realize that I was assuming erroneously that the Act and Samoan families existed on the same continuum, the Act offering the bare skeleton that the families fleshed out. The Samoan social worker was gently correcting me and trying to help me understand the specific form of mediation that he had to do. Social workers must take implicit and unarticulated aspects of Samoan family life and transfigure these into explicit topics for conflict resolution within the parameters established by the Act. At the same time, they must contend with the ways in which the Act invokes family systems that reinscribe nuclear family dynamics. The legislation often presumes an egalitarian circulation of knowledge and resources, alongside an emphasis on the parent-child relationship as the primary relationship, thus imagining extended families through a culturally specific nuclear family lens.

In this chapter, I turn to the different approaches to the parent-child relationship inherent in the CYPF Act and among the Samoan families I encountered to detail the gap between the families implied in the Act and the actual Samoan families encountering the Act's bureaucratic transformations. For both Samoans and New Zealand legislators and social workers, the parent-child relationship was the central relationship for understanding how to bring children into larger social unities—be it transnational Samoan communities or the New Zealand nation. For both, the parent-child relationship also provided insights into how and when people were cultural. In addition, both used the same relationship

---

1. Because of the exigencies of fieldwork, I never had a tape recorder during these discussions. As a result, I am relying on my field notes, rather than a verbatim transcript.

to articulate substantively different assumptions about what it means to belong to a family and to belong to other social unities.

Kinship theorists have long known that certain kin relations are particularly conducive for articulating the paradoxes of belonging to a given social order. Some kin relations embody the productive tensions built into particular forms of sociality better than others. For example, Meyer Fortes (1949) discusses how the Tallensi's version of patrilineality made father-son relationships a central locus for tensions surrounding jural or economic group membership. These relationships become more than metaphors for addressing the tensions in being social in particular ways. They become magnets for anxious practices and anxious talk as people use these relationships to explore what it means to belong to a specific group. For the Samoan families I spoke with, as well as for the New Zealand social services representatives I interviewed, the parent-child relationship was the vehicle for thinking about how resources and information should flow within the family. However, the assumptions underlying these distributions were substantively different, leading to miscommunications and involved negotiations at the sites where Samoan families met New Zealand government bureaucracy.

What It Means to Be a Parent

Readers familiar with other anthropological accounts of Samoan kinship may be surprised that I have singled out the parent-child relationship as the one through which migrant families understand their Samoan obligations. Ethnographers of independent Samoa and American Samoa have long agreed with other kinship theorists that there are some familial bonds that Samoans will use to reflect on the connections between groups and their members (cf. Schoeffel 1978, 1999; Shore 1981; Tcherkézoff 1993). These ethnographers have focused on the sister-brother tie as the relationship whose structure metaphorically reflects the ways in which people practice Samoan sociality. In the following two sections, I will describe the transition sparked by migration from a focus on the sister-brother tie to the parent-child bond. In the process, I continue discussing a recurring theme: the ways in which resources and knowledge circulate within

Samoan migrant families, practices that New Zealand government agencies have difficulty addressing.

When ethnographers describe the sister-brother bond as a powerfully metaphorical relationship for Samoans, they are describing an ideological relationship that can serve as an ordering principle for the daily negotiations of contradictory hierarchies. In Samoa, people experience social organization as a cluster of hierarchies that interweave, sometimes discordantly, and define the appropriate displays of respect and competition as the contexts shift. Walking through a Samoan village, a Samoan man might have to show proper deference to a church minister, another family's *matai,* his older sister, and his paternal grandfather's brother. Age, gender, degree of relatedness, and chiefly status all contribute to determining the exact nature of any given social relationship. The *matai* system principally structures the hierarchical relationships on a village level. Within families, the hierarchical relationships are made quite visible at meal-times, when the *matai* and elders of the family are served first, then the adult family members, the children, and finally the daughter-in-laws of the household. Yet, if the daughter-in-law is a foreigner or is married to the only son in the family who is a minister, she might be served with the other siblings. The status of foreigner or minister's wife is honored along different hierarchical axes other than husband-wife relations, and the different hierarchical expectations can collide at meals. While every social relationship in Samoa is hierarchical, not every hierarchical relationship is aligned neatly or consistently vis-à-vis the other hierarchical relationships.

When anthropologists have discussed this tension between hierarchies, they have turned to Samoan concepts of gender as a telling site (Schoeffel 1978, 1999; Shore 1981; Tcherkézoff 1993). They have focused on the fact that in Samoa, a person's sex does not determine his or her status in a particular context. Rather, the dominant social relationship in a given setting will decide the hierarchical structure of the event, and thus a person's status. Samoan constructions of gender present a common and apt example of how hierarchical relationships in Samoa are all inherently contextual. All three anthropologists mentioned above agree that in Samoa, husband-wife relationships are substantively different from sister-brother relationships. Samoan wives invariably owe respect to their husbands and, when with their husband's family, are obligated to serve by performing the household chores: preparing meals, cleaning, and eating last (Schoeffel 1979).

Wives are subservient to their affines. By contrast, Samoan sisters, in relation to brothers, must do much less when with their families because they are embodying a role owed respect and obedience and, in general, are representing the family's honor (Schoeffel 1978, 308; Shore 1981, 200). Brothers could not say inappropriate things around their sisters, they could not share clothes, and there are many other avoidance practices brothers and sisters had to perform to show respect for each other. Thus a woman is either a wife or a sister. She is always defined in terms of a dyadic relationship. Gender is not based on a contrast between men and women, but rather on a contrast between husband-wife and sister-brother (Schoeffel 1978; Tcherkézoff 1993). The husband-wife tie is not a social relationship on the same order as the sister-brother link because the sister-brother link is *the* core metaphorical relationship of Samoan kinship. Thus when a woman moves from being a sister-brother to a husband-wife, she is moving between ways in which social relationships can channel expressions of power.

While each scholar disagrees about the precise nature of the dyadic relationships, all agree about the basic Samoan structural interaction between power and social relationships. All three scholars argue that the *feagaiga*—the dyadic power relationship modeled most frequently on the sister-brother tie—is a metaphorical vehicle for understanding Samoans' experiences of Samoan society as a totality. For these anthropologists, the relationship between the sister and brother in Samoa is a microcosm of the larger social macrocosm. In addition, in Samoa, power is never embodied wholly in one person. Power is inherently dyadic, with each person in the relationship embodying one pole. *Feagaiga* relationships—between sisters and brothers, high chiefs and talking chiefs, or ministers and God—embody this distinction. In the most abstract form, power is expressed in a passive and active form, with, for example, the sister as an instantiation of the passive form of power and the brother as the active form, or the high chief as the passive form and the talking chief as the active form. Enacting this bond is metaphorically enacting the fundamentals of the larger Samoan social order.

While ideologically some hierarchical relationships may be privileged over others, this does not necessarily serve as a practical guideline for Samoans navigating their daily life. Context by context, people are constantly juggling their different hierarchical roles. A child could easily be in a quagmire in a given moment, trying to figure out which of two mutually exclusive requests to fulfill—the minister's request or her father's sister's request. Douglass St. Christian (1994) captured this tension elegantly in the following passage:

> A command from one authority can be superseded by a command from another, and obligations to one powerful figure can be overruled by obligations to some other. As such, obedience in any context is premised on a calculation of how accepting the authority of person X relates to, and effects, conditions of obligation and obedience to persons Y and Z. This web of potential sites of command and obedience also opens up a wide field of strategic disobedience. (156)

In lived experience, the differing hierarchies are experienced as contradictory demands that must be negotiated. So while the *feagaiga* may be Samoan society's self-reflexive relationship, through which people can experience Samoan society as a particular type of totality, in practice this knowledge is continually juxtaposed with daily fragmented enactments of hierarchies.

Migrating Hierarchies

While the brother-sister relationship may be a useful relationship for exploring what it means to be Samoan in Samoa, after migration, Samoans have tended to explore this issue through the parent-child relationship. In Samoa, people are continually negotiating a constellation of hierarchies; while hierarchy itself is not up for grabs, the particular configurations are. Not so surprisingly, different hierarchies are privileged after migration. At the family level, the *feagaiga* is no longer practiced as systematically. Brothers and sisters discuss each other's love lives openly, share clothes readily, and no longer allocate chores as they did in Samoa. And the brother-sister relationship no longer serves as the self-descriptive relationship for Samoan society, the familial metaphor that guides people into understanding how power and sociality are channeled and articulated. Instead, it has become just another Samoan hierarchical relationship that migrants must manage.

I was chatting in the Samoan Congregational church hall in Wellington one day, watching with a married woman as the unmarried young girls began serving food to the minister and elders of the church. I told this woman that it didn't seem to me as though the younger generation practices the *feagaiga* anymore. She agreed, and then, with humor and succinctness, said: "The boys are just like their fathers now. They lie around the house with their legs up and their 'things' up." In one sentence, she managed to convey two significant ways in which the *feagaiga* has lapsed. The young men no longer perform the regular gendered chores that encapsulate a brother-sister division. Second, for the young men the expression of sexuality has become more dominant than an expression of respect.

Practicing the *feagaiga* has not gone completely out of fashion. One instance in which the *feagaiga* still holds occurs when people are watching television. Several young adults told me that they still can't watch romantic scenes on television if their cross-sex siblings (but also parents) are in the room. They change the channel the moment it looks as though the actors might kiss. While channel switching is a sign of respect for one's cross-sex sibling, it is not a sign of respect reserved only for that relationship. Other avoidance practices that were reserved only for sisters and brothers are no longer practiced in diaspora; for example, sisters and brothers in the United States will share clothes without anyone commenting when it was shameful to do so in Samoa.

In many ways, the relationship that has replaced the sister-brother bond for migrants is the parent-child relationship. While the parent-child bond doesn't have the same role as the sister-brother link, it is becoming the relationship through which migrants articulate their links to Samoa and Samoanness. The relationship with parents has become the foci for thinking about Samoanness in two ways: in terms of transmitting knowledge and managing resources. How people know what to do in Samoan contexts, how they learn what behaviors are typically Samoan, or how they decide how to spend their money and time—all these issues become linked to the parent-child relationship after migration.

The parent-child relationship articulates Samoanness in different ways, depending on whether a person was raised in Samoa. In Samoa, children learn expected behavior from a wide variety of people, partially as a by-product of the multiple hierarchical relationships people are constantly navigating (Ochs 1988). In New Zealand, parents become the main conduit through which children learn how to be Samoan. Parents become a much more important source for teaching appropriate behavior than they were in Samoa, and several of my New Zealand–raised friends described how they learned about Samoan practices from their parents or grandparents.

Just as often, however, I was told about how strained the learning process became. New Zealand–raised Samoans told me that their parents seemed to expect them to know what to do automatically, and when they made a mistake, the parents would criticize them publicly. My research assistant, who was raised in New Zealand, wrote a journal entry outlining this dynamic as she experienced it:

> I am remembering back to when I was a child and how difficult it was to understand my mother wanted me to do something. She wouldn't say anything instead she would look at me as if I automatically knew what she wanted. An example of this would probably be when I was in primary school we had visitors arrive and I continued to watch television. She glared at me as if I had done something wrong, because I didn't click she said aloud in front of the visitors, "This is the problem with children born in New Zealand they don't know how to do any *'feau'* [chores]. They can only watch television and play outside." I stared at her stunned and highly embarrassed, she growled me to get up and fix something for the visitors.

As a result of similar experiences, many New Zealand–raised Samoans experienced Samoan practices as implicit and rigid expectations that their parents' generation seemed to grasp intuitively and expected them to do as well. Thus, from the New Zealand–raised children's perspective, their Samoan parents often represented a canonical body of social knowledge, a static set of precepts and traditions that all Samoan-raised people understood.

While Samoan-raised migrants do not share the New Zealand–raised anxieties about their parents, the structure of *fa'alavelave* (Samoan ritual exchanges) ensures that their relationships with their parents become the relationship with which they think about their connection to Samoa. Even the ways in which migrants decide how much to donate for a *fa'alavelave* reinforces this shift. In my interviews, my interlocutors described two basic patterns for determining how much to give and to whom. In some instances, the *matai* (which in migration was a parent, or a parent's oldest local sibling) of the New Zealand branch of the family learns that one of their relatives soon will be having a funeral or a wedding. The *matai* decides how much he or she would like the family as a whole to donate and then calls up each family member and tells them how much to give. Occasionally the *matai* simply tells the family members that a *fa'alavelave* is looming and asks them to "give as much as you can afford." If the *matai* can't collect a sufficient amount of money, he or she will (as most informed me) supplement the amount with an even larger personal donation so that the family is not shamed in the exchange. Alternatively, a parent (who is often the *matai* of the family as well) will call a family meeting, and family members will determine how much the parents and sibling set as a unit will contribute to their family branch's donation. *Fa'alavelave* are the typical reason for family meetings.

I have never had the opportunity to attend a family meeting, but I have heard several renditions of what occurs within these family meetings. To the degree that it is possible to generalize, I have noticed two themes emerging from people's accounts. First, not everyone can speak freely. Certain people (such as affines) don't have the right to speak at all, and often aren't even present. In addition, parents will make the final decision, determining how much money is given and how much each of their children will contribute. In short, the private techniques with which money and fine mats are gathered for a *fa'alavelave* are part of the hierarchical relationships that shape family dynamics. *Fa'alavelave*, as mentioned in chapter 1, are the primary vehicle through which Samoan migrants experience their connection and commitment to *fa'asamoa* (the Samoan way). The parent-child relationship becomes the relationship through which to connect to *fa'asamoa*. Meanwhile the practices that affirm the *feagaiga* between brothers and sisters go by the wayside. The shift only grows stronger as Samoan migrant brothers and sisters increasingly share clothes and work out at gyms together.

In short, for Samoan migrants, the parent-child relationship has become the central relationship for thinking about how children connect to larger social unities. This shift, however, has not substantively changed what it means to be part of a Samoan family. The emphasis is still on how people are contributing to the ways in which Samoan families locate themselves in larger social unities such as church communities, local neighborhoods, or villages in Samoa. The emphasis on the parent-child relationship from a Samoan perspective is not on how an internally focused family nurtures its own children into independence. Rather, the emphasis is outward, on how children will contribute to the family's connections with other families and other communities. The ways in which people have restructured their Samoan networks for exchanging information and resources in migration do not reflect the techniques or priorities that the government agencies imagine for families.

Between Governments and Families

Both government agencies and Samoan migrant families stress the parent-child relationship, yet for different reasons. For government agencies, children are supposed to grow independent. For Samoan migrant families, this independence is fraught with the potential for a destructive assimilation that they struggle to prevent. This gap becomes an issue when New Zealand government social workers intervene in bureaucratically determined cases of child abuse or juvenile delinquency among Samoan families. (A U.S. example is discussed in the next chapter.)

In New Zealand parliamentary debates, parents and children were often discussed alongside terms referring to social unities, such as family or community. These terms were often consciously used as strategically deployed shifters; that is, terms that have different definitions and uses in different contexts. Bonnie Urciuoli (2003) describes a *strategically deployed shifter* as "a lexical item or expression deployed in different discursive fields so that, in effect, people using term X in a referring expression in field A are engaged in a different pragmatic activity from those using the formally identical term X in a referring expression in field B" (396).

Families and communities have become strategically deployable shifters in the New Zealand parliamentary context largely because of a long history of political arguments that families and communities are culturally different. Over time, Māori members of Parliament have successfully compelled other legislators to become aware that these social unities do not have universal forms. Families are not defined along the same lines by all social groups, and thus what "family" actually refers to is generally understood to be indeterminate. Michael Cullen, then Deputy Labour Prime

Minister of New Zealand, is quite explicit that this understanding lies at heart of the new Act, and he also responds to an Opposition member's derision about the ways terms are resolutely not defined:

MICHAEL CULLEN: The term "family" has to be widely defined in the New Zealand context. It cannot be defined purely in terms of the traditional nuclear family; it has to include *iwi, hapu,* and *whanau.*

MAURICE MCTIGUE: What's an *iwi?*

MICHAEL CULLEN: The member for Timaru may laugh about what an *iwi* is. I suggest that he do some reading very quickly. He will find it very helpful for him in understanding some of the key issues in New Zealand politics in society over the next 20 years. The family has to consider the different cultural patterns within society. That is not sickly white liberalism; it is simply recognising the differing social patterns in our society.

It is no accident that Maurice McTigue's interjection centers on Māori definitions of social unities; this is precisely the bone of contention that Māori members of parliament have introduced into political debates. And Michael Cullen's response is telling as well: the legislation that members of Parliament were fashioning was consciously meant to describe vaguely defined social unities as a way to respond to a multicultural population.

The members of Parliament (MPs) were aware that legislation required that people be explicit about social unities in ways that invariably misrepresented how the social unities were in fact organized. In discussing a bill that allowed non–kin-based groups to care for children, Bob Simcock, a National MP, said: "Leadership in all communities is largely informal. It becomes formal only when the State has to have a relationship with it, and therefore has to define it and put it in a box. In doing so, the State almost always misrepresents it, and almost always misdefines. But that is the way legislation needs to be because the only way the Crown can relate to an entity other than an individual is to define it in some way" (New Zealand Parliamentary Debates [N.Z.P.D.], March 2, 2000). Simcock describes how the language of legislation generates particular problems when thinking about social unities, that the State often requires that social unities behave as though they are individuals and will use legal definitions to formulate social unities as individual-like entities. He also points out that terms indexing social unities have different pragmatic uses in different contexts. As these excerpts attest, MPs were aware not only that they were using strategically defined shifters but also that the legal phrasing invariably changes people's ways to refer to social unities.

In general, MPs agreed not to ask for detailed definitions of what is a family and instead focused on how families, communities, parents, and children should be encouraged to interact through legislation. Yet, while speakers in Parliament widely recognize that families and communities are strategically deployed shifters, they do not often acknowledge that for some, families and communities are processes, not already bounded unities. The legislative intent was to allow for a plurality of social relationships to count as family—ranging from Pakeha (Euro-New Zealand) nuclear families to various forms of extended families. The MPs drafting this Act made two fundamental assumptions in an attempt to legislate for such diversity.

First, they presumed that all families function with common aims. While there may be multiple paths toward the same goal, each family has, as its foundational purpose, the function of caring for the needs and well being of each of its members. There may be different kinds of families, but the families have the same basic priorities. They simply attempt to fulfill their goals by alternative methods. Government officials also understood this, as I found out while discussing a new government project, "Strengthening Families" with a New Zealand public relations officer of a local social welfare office. I asked her how her agency was defining families, and she said that the definition was as broad as possible. I asked what it meant to belong to a category so broadly defined, and she explained that families were similar to her family, a team, with every member contributing his or her fair share. According to her, it is possible to see all families as paths leading to good citizens.

Second, this perspective assumed that families are social unities in which every member contributes to ensuring that the unity stays functional. From this perspective, families are dysfunctional when members do not cooperate toward a common goal of ensuring that the family as a unity satisfies the needs of each of its members. This form of unity emerges from visions of how nuclear families should operate, in which, as a corollary, family conflict is negative and an indication of dysfunction.

Parents, children, families, communities—all were terms that parliamentarians thought were preexisting entities that could be addressed in legislation. What legislation was supposed to delineate was the ways in which these preexisting social unities should be interacting to best care for New Zealand's children. Members of Parliament invariably suggested that shifting units of scale could resolve problems children faced. When parents fail, extended families should step in, and when extended families fail, then communities should. How extended families or communities were internally organized was left vague, but they were all too often the solution to parental or familial failures. Liane Dalziel, a Labour MP, provides a typical rhetorical move in the following speech:

> Part of the Government's problem in this area is summed up in the explanatory note to this Bill. It focuses on the much-lauded Strengthening Families programme, but there is a fallacy in the Government's approach. That fallacy is that we cannot strengthen families without strengthening the communities within which those families live. To coin a phrase, no family is an island. Yet this Government has abandoned communities to their own limited resources and isolated families in the process—and now we blame those families. For children and young people to thrive, we need to rebuild communities so that families are supported and the children are nurtured within them. [N.Z.P.D. June 1, 1999]

Here communities, loosely defined, should become the supporting infrastructure enabling families to care for their children. In all cases, the focus is on how best to care for children, with parents, families, and communities all acting as potential caregivers, implicitly all given agency and responsibility as though they were individuals. The parent-child relationship is the model for all other relationships between relatives and the child, or for larger social unities and the child. So what are the assumptions about the parent-child relationship that is then presumed for all relationships?

In the parliamentary view of the family, all family members are working toward a common goal, a functioning family, in which hierarchy primarily emerges in the parent-child relationship. MPs tended to assume that families are comprised of individuals who adopt certain roles. Family roles themselves are mixtures of emotion and convention, in which society provides the forms through which individuals can express the affectionate emotions they feel toward their relatives. As the parliamentary debate over a 1991 Child Support Bill illustrates, there is an implicit anxiety over people's relationships to their familial roles. For example, the role of father is both circumscribed by expected emotions and actions, and presented as a choice. However this choice is presented as potentially a dangerous one, especially when commitments to other relationships might intervene. Fathers theoretically choose to adopt the conventions of parenthood. But there is a possibility that a father might choose against parenthood, and this would be a destructive choice. To safeguard against fatherhood's potential hazards, the government must pass appropriate legislation. Judith Tizard, an MP from Panmure, captures this in her speech in Parliament on August 22, 1991:

> While I believe that this system [the new legislation] will be fairer I know that many second wives or wives who have married men who already have children feel resentful about the amount that they have to contribute to the children of the earlier marriage. It is often a difficult position [for the women who feel resentful]. One of the points that I want the select committee to consider carefully is where the fairness lies. A constituent recently told me that because his wife had formed another relationship he had been forced out of his marriage and out of his relationship with his children, and that he was deeply resentful and saw no reason for maintaining his wife's choice. While he was perfectly prepared to take responsibility for his children, he was not prepared to do anything to assist his former wife. (N.Z.P.D August 22, 1991, 4393)

Tizard describes the newly configured relationships in terms of how each member chooses to love or contribute. Feeling compelled to nurture rather than choosing freely to do so becomes a dilemma for anyone in this vision of the family. Tizard is suggesting a characteristic of a kinship system composed of individual choosers that Marilyn Strathern unpacked for English kinship: "If the modern person is a microcosm of anything, it is of *the socialising or domesticating process* itself. The person registers the effect of culture on nature, society on the individual, and is in this sense convention (partially) embodied but never of course convention (fully) realized" (1991, 125). In short, people are not their roles; instead they are in a state of perpetually choosing to become their roles.

With the exception of the child, this choice takes place under the guise of two types of equality: originary and distributive. First, the assumption, regardless of contradicting circumstances, is that people freely choose to be part of a family, but that a naturalized affection makes the pro-family choice inevitable. The choice emerges out of an imagined originary equality, a space without power relations informing the choice. The second form of equality is the one imagined after choice, and it is as idealized. This is the equality of distribution, in which every family member is presumed to have an equal voice deciding how money is allocated, as well as equitable needs. This originary space of equality is a crucial assumption for understanding the mediation process in the Family Group Conference, which is central to the Act.

This approach encourages certain presuppositions that elide kinship rather than engaging with different forms of relatedness as structuring principles. As Robin Fleming (1997) points out, policy makers believe that resources circulate among members of the household, and the central priority is presumably to ensure that the resources are used for household members' basic needs first. Each household member has basic needs that should be met with the resources available to any member of the household. Surplus, if there is surplus, should ideally go to the younger members of the household. This creates the context for government officials to read certain dynamics as problems. One of the major tensions that this approach predicts is that when people spend resources at their disposal for their own self-interest, and on items considered luxuries (and often illicit luxuries), not necessities, there will be conflict within the family.[2] Muriel Newman, a conservative ACT MP, laid out this perspective in the following speech, in which she was critiquing the government's welfare policy during a discussion of an amendment to the CYPF Act:

> The reality is that dysfunctional families are often very poor managers of their money, as well as poor managers of much of the rest of their lives. All too often the welfare money does get spent on alcohol, drugs, and gambling. When there is little left over for food and other necessities, then that is when people go to the foodbanks or get welfare emergency assistance grants. That is not what we want to be promoting. We do not want to see irresponsibility. The other day I spoke to a church minister who said that basically his

---

2. As I mentioned in chapter 1, while spending money to form one's individual consumer identity can also be a source of tension among Samoan families, this was not how the tension concerning spending money was expressed to me. For the most part, Samoan people I interviewed talked about balancing their household's economic needs against the demands of their extended families.

church was sick of giving out food parcels to people who had spent their welfare money on drugs, gambling, and so on. His church members were sick of going around to homes to help and seeing Sky television [satellite television] and cellphones. That shows the strange system we have that provides Government assistance to help with the necessities of life, such as food, clothing, and so on. If families do not have the right sense of responsibility, that money can be used on other things, and in fact all too often children are the ones who miss out. [N.Z.P.D., June 1, 1999]

For Muriel Newman, and many others in the New Zealand Parliament, families are supposed to allocate resources so that the basic needs of the household members are always taken care of first, and the family is dysfunctional if it does not.

The relationship between parents and children is a marked exception to this ethos of familial equality, partially because, from a parliamentary perspective, families' central function is to socialize the children into being productive citizens. Becoming a productive citizen also entails becoming independent from one's family of origin. From this standpoint, the central tension within a family is between the parent and the child, in which the child is continually attempting to reach a level of independence against the backdrop of the parent's attempts to instruct the child properly. According to Strathern, parents will represent the unified sociality against which children forge their independence. "Parents already united in a relationship produce individual children. We might further say that their unity as one person presupposes the individuality of the child" (Strathern 1991, 15). The parent-child relationship is a momentary hierarchical stage in the child's progress toward becoming an equal member of their own family.

Parents do not struggle for independence from their children; the quest for independence flows only in one direction. As a result, these children are seen as the withholders of information. They don't tell their parents who their friends are, what they do in school, how involved they are in drugs. It is the parent's responsibility to uncover this information; they must attempt to understand what is happening in their child's life by forging communicative ties that will encourage the necessary flow of information. Of course, the opposite is not true. The child is not expected to know about the travails of the parent's life, and in fact this type of knowledge is often seen as inappropriate. Other family relationships are not seen as highly charged in terms of the circulation of knowledge.

Information ideally circulates within the family freely and easily. This assumption led to one of the most commonly repeated critiques of the CYPF bill. Opponents of the bill, and in particular of Family Group Conferences, argued that this bill was enabling dysfunctional families to perpetuate established patterns of abuse. Mr. Jim Gerard put this argument succinctly, although other MPs, such as V. S. Young and Katherine O'Regan, made similar objections.

> MR. GERARD: The Opposition is concerned that the radical proposals in the Bill—described by some as trail-blazing—may not work. There is no basis for the family, as well as the social worker, to be the only decision-making body. Opposition members are not opposed to family involvement—quite the opposite. That is already happening more and more. We are not opposed to the need for cultural sensitivity—that is happening now within child protection teams throughout the country. However, we are concerned at violence towards children, particularly within the family. It is regrettable that in about 80 percent of cases of physical or sexual violence within the family both parents know about it. Therefore it is difficult to believe that, together with the Department of Social Welfare, families will solve the problem they have been hiding in the first place, in which the child is the victim.

In this and other speeches, the bill's supposition that families are essentially well-meaning and competent was hotly contested by the bill's opponents. They claimed that the Act would require dysfunctional families to continue caring for the children that the family was harming. Gerard's objection is based on an assumption about how knowledge circulates within families. Knowledge is supposed to be distributed equally between all the adults, or at least, any information necessary to make decisions about the running of the family will be distributed equally. Secrecy is seen as destructive and is normally associated with disruptive activities that are meant to prioritize individual pleasures over family needs or boundaries, practices such as adultery or drug use. Intriguingly in these objections, child abuse is understood to be known by all family members and implicitly condoned.

All the parliamentarians, those in support of the bill as well as those opposed, presume that families act as cohesive units for information transmission and resource management. There is a belief that any adult member of a household, and often a teenager, will serve as a liaison in terms of information transmission. When the social worker tells one parent the court procedures by which a juvenile delinquent is tried, he or she is supposedly telling all the responsible people in the family. Anyone can represent that family and carry the necessary knowledge back and forth to all the other members. The principle tension surrounding information flow, from this perspective, emerges from the family's central project—to form productive citizens. This is not the case for Samoan families, where information does not flow smoothly between siblings, spouses, or across any generation gap. Indeed, most, if not all, of the relationships in Samoan families are highly charged in terms of knowledge transmission, although the types of tensions vary from relationship to relationship.

For European New Zealanders, a main goal of all families is to raise children properly. They think of families as household systems in which members continually struggle with their dependence on the family as a group and independence as individuals. From this perspective, the family is imagined to circulate knowledge and resources as a coordinated and unified group. As a result, these policy makers often imagine extended families through a nuclear family lens. As I discussed earlier, from a Samoan perspective, unity is only periodically desired or achieved. Samoan migrant families have different goals, such as making the family visible as a collective that can gather together ample resources for ritual exchanges. When New Zealand's social welfare departments have Samoan families as clients, the Samoan ways of practicing family unity exposes the nuclear family biases within the CYPF Act. In short, when people engaged with the CYPF Act, both social workers and parliamentarians, assume that Samoan extended families function as certain types of unities, they are making the intricacies of Samoan kinship practices invisible.

Family Conferences

The hallmark innovation introduced by the CYPF (Children, Young Persons, and Their Families) Act, as mentioned above, is the Family Group Conference, in which all the people involved meet together to decide how best to administer to the child's needs. The family conferences are geared toward creating a forum in which family members and other interested people can, under the guidance of a CYF (Children, Youth, and Families) social worker, develop a plan to protect and support the minor. In the case of juvenile crime, the emphasis is on ensuring that the youth makes restitution, both to the victim and to the government. By introducing Family Group Conferences, the government took an explicit stance on the essential good will of all families. The bill states that "given the resources, the information, and the power, a family group will generally make safe and appropriate decisions for children" (CYPF Act 1989: 3). In short, the ostensible purpose of the act is to reconfigure the dynamics between government and family, with government rejecting the role of savior. While government officials still intervene when families appear to fail to uphold their side of the division of labor, social workers are only supposed to create a forum for families to develop their own solutions to the institutionally defined problems. The premise is that families are basically functional unities that circulate information and resources in such a way that the needs of the individual members are met. Failure, from this perspective, occurs because of a breakdown in these flows, which social workers can mend by creating an arena for the family to heal itself.

Through the generosity of counselors at a Samoan nonprofit organization, I had the opportunity to attend a few counseling sessions with mothers who had been involved with Family Group Conferences. The organization treated these clients because the local CYF workers had sought culturally appropriate treatment for the clients and did not have available Samoan social workers on staff in that office. I watched the aftermath of these conferences, and for reasons of confidentiality and bureaucracy, never witnessed an actual conference. But the tell-tale traces of mismatch still lingered for months afterward. I will summarize the details of one typical case, which captures the ways in which the intricacies of kinship do not translate.

This was an unusual case for me to observe in one respect because I had some forewarning about the underlying issues. In other instances, I had no advance warning about the facts of a case before observing a session. Normally, as the first counseling session would unfold, I would be struggling to decipher the shared narratives that had already been established. In this case, the Samoan counselor, Lupe, had told me some of her general concerns for her client prior to the counseling session, although she described the circumstances without telling me which client it was. It did not take me long to match her abstracted accounts to the person I was meeting in the first session. Before I met the client, I knew that her counselor saw this case as one of the tragedies of migration. The mother, Rita, had three children, each of whom had been removed by CYF, one by one. Lupe did not think that she was a bad mother, simply unsophisticated. Lupe said that Rita took care of her children's basic needs, ensuring that they were clothed and fed. But she had no understanding of their emotional needs and was not careful about who she let into the house and who she turned away. She had her children in her teens, which Lupe felt would not have been a problem if she had stayed in Samoa. There, Rita's mother or another older female relative would have been able to supplement the skills that she lacked. But in New Zealand, she was expected to display the full range of parenting skills. Lupe explained with a gentle sigh that Rita acted as though she was her children's older sister, not their mother. Lupe wished that her client had just one older relative in New Zealand, but that had not been the pattern of her family's migration. Instead, she was the oldest in her sibling set in New Zealand. Because of Samoan family hierarchy, her younger siblings had no authority to take over some of her parenting responsibilities or to control the flow of guests into her house.

Rita was in her late twenties, was hesitant and soft-spoken, and never initiated a conversation or line of thought. She only responded to Lupe's gentle questioning, and as the questions slowly built one upon the other, a story of communication gaps began to emerge. She wanted her children to visit over Christmas, but these were not the arrangements that had been made for her. Her younger sister, in violation of Samoan family hierarchical principles, had made arrangements with the CYF social worker for the children to visit Rita two weeks before Christmas. Rita wasn't allowed to be with her children unsupervised; the younger sister or other relatives had to be present. As Lupe continued asking about the arrangements, it became apparent that Lupe had been negotiating with both the social worker and the sister for permission for the children to spend Christmas dinner with their mother. Lupe had been making all sorts of tentative schedules, with everyone's knowledge but the client's. The client had been kept in the dark about this likely change in plans. It was only in the way that Lupe kept asking questions that this alternative was gradually revealed to Rita.

This case contains many of the consequences of a clash between forms of systemic explicitness created when Samoan families must respond to CYF policy. First, Lupe was constantly forced to teach her client to regard mothering as a problematic arena to which she must consciously tend. The client did not think that mothering required any form of self-reflexivity and hence found the reasons for her children's removal hard to fathom. Second, the client was suffering from a hierarchy spread across too much geographical distance. She had no larger structures of authority, in the guise of older relatives, to turn to in New Zealand. As a result, she was expected to be a parent who managed all parental responsibilities, instead of having them distributed among an extended family. Finally, the information that formed the basis for most decisions circulated in an unpredictable fashion from a CYF perspective. The mother did not know plans for herself or her children and had little say in the matter. Rather than assuming, as CYF does, that it was transparent who knew what, and when, this was precisely what the Samoan counselor had to establish. She was using the counseling sessions to ensure flows of information that her contractor, CYF, took for granted.

Knowledge plays a revelatory role in the implicit narrative of how families function. For New Zealand social workers, one of the major causes of dysfunctionality is sheer ignorance: if people knew better, they would manage their families properly. Thus social workers are cast in the roles of bringing transformative knowledge; once everyone in the family knows the same things, the family can start functioning properly again. At times, this is expressed in slightly different terms—that families are unaware of the services the government can offer to assist them in their efforts to resolve crises. Families would access government resources if only they knew about them. In these cases, social workers are information brokers, the nodes through which families can enter into the government agencies' flow of resources and information.

Alongside this assumption is the belief that in Family Group Conferences, people are interacting on an equal playing field, and everyone has an opportunity to speak and be heard. Family Group Conferences are meant to re-create ritually each person's commitment to the family as a functioning system, while giving them the opportunity to articulate their own needs, which the family is expected to satisfy. This takes place in a context where everyone is presumed equal, and presumed to be actively choosing to participate in the family. This presumption of equality is, as I discussed, antithetical to the way people structure their Samoan relationships. Samoan family meetings, which CYF family group conferences are supposedly modeled on, are not sites for asserting a baseline equality. On the contrary, Samoan family meetings are contexts in which the hierarchies of who gets to speak and for whom is challenged and reasserted. Family meetings are attended by members of the extended family in that city and occasionally a sibling set's affines. The meetings can be moments for airing and delaying well-established tensions. Often, these are situations in which people can negotiate the details of various ongoing conflicts, even shifting the conflict's trajectory without resolving it. My interlocutors presumed neither family unity nor individual equality in these settings. From a Samoan perspective, the work of kinship is to express different forms of hierarchy—of hotly contested public unity that is an achievement precisely because of the private conflicts.

New Zealand parliamentarians were conscious of some of the problems in legislating for cultural families. They attempted to write legislation with units so vaguely defined that no cultural approach to being a family was penalized. Despite the authors' efforts, my Samoan interlocutors kept finding that the implied families in the CYPF Act were quite different from the actual families in which they lived. The Act presumes that all families share a common project—raising children to be productive citizens.[3] From this perspective, cultures are the many avenues for reaching a common goal. As long as the families can appear to agree with the principal tenet that families are all focused on child rearing, legislative acts such as CYPF (1989) could try to accommodate diversity. When, as is the case with many Samoan families, transnational exchange—not child rearing—is widely viewed as the primary labor of families, a conflict between diversity and nationhood emerges. The families no longer share the same project as the nation-state, and becoming Samoan is not the road to being a productive citizen.

This tension becomes most evident in the different ways that the New Zealand MPs and my Samoan interlocutors found talking about the parent-child relationship to be useful for articulating what they each perceived as the problems of being cultural. For the NZ MPs, they saw all relationships between authority figures and a child as metaphorically

---

3. While in New Zealand the common goal of families is supposed to be child rearing, this is not an integral goal for nation-states. It is just as possible for nation-states to expect all families to care for the elderly. It is not the content of the goal that is integral for liberal democracies, although the content does determine bureaucratic structures.

grounded in the parent-child relationship. This means that non–kin-based organizations, schools, and all kin had some version of parental responsibility toward children. For Samoan migrants, children were enmeshed in many different hierarchical relationships, not all were variants or derivative of the parent-child relationship. This provided the seeds for longstanding historical misunderstandings that the CYPF Act was intended to remedy by no longer insisting that government agencies were to be parents to children when their own parents failed them. The CYPF Act was suggested when the public debates about biculturalism made it apparent that 1970s and '80s government solutions to family problems would ensure cultural clashes. Being explicit about culture and cultural difference in New Zealand meant eventually that family legislation had to recognize families and communities as providing their own culturally appropriate solutions to their members' problems. Yet this recognition did not make apparent the ways in which government legislation and bureaucracy was being framed as acultural. Instead, the legislation's own implicit assumptions about how families should operate were taken as the unmarked norm.

It is this silence about how the acultural is constructed in the same breath as the cultural that Samoan community workers were rejecting when they told me that they had to bring the Act and the families onto the same level. When the Samoan community workers did this, they were reframing the Act, explicitly framing as cultural what the authors of the Act saw as acultural. The Samoan community workers were declaring in no uncertain terms that the presuppositions of nuclear families embedded in the Act were cultural presuppositions. Thus, from the Samoan community workers' perspective, the legislation was erroneously offering as unmarked and acultural the very cultural solution that children should always be paramount. And the Act was proposing this to families for whom being explicitly cultural means making *fa'alavelave* paramount, in which family hierarchies were far more intricate than those in the Act's imagined families. Despite the legislators' efforts to create culturally sensitive forms for family conflict resolution, Samoan social workers and community counselors had to translate the Act for Samoan families, negotiating and managing the conflicting presuppositions of what it means to be a nuclear family embedded in the Act and what it means to be an extended family for Samoans.

5

CONSTRUCTING CHOICE, COMPELLING CULTURE

Throughout this book, I argue that people's reflexive understandings are crucial to understanding the ways people are cultural or acultural in certain circumstances. In this chapter, I want to turn to a familiar analytical concept in migration studies, assimilation, and ask how focusing on reflexivity changes how analyses of assimilation unfold. When one begins with reflexivity, assimilation becomes a differently charged question. For starters, assimilation is not the stereotypical given that all migrants should achieve as quickly as possible for their own self-interest. Even the term *assimilation* itself becomes misleading as a way to think through diasporic experiences. Instead, one asks when people are using assimilation themselves to understand their experiences of diaspora.

This chapter is about something that surprised me quite a bit when I moved from doing fieldwork in New Zealand to doing fieldwork in mainland United States. When Samoan community workers in San Francisco started describing to me how Samoan parents needed to be taught to adapt their parenting techniques to the exigencies of living in the United States, my first thought was—how odd, no one in New Zealand would claim that. In New Zealand, people would tell me that the children needed to be taught Samoan culture, not that the parents needed to be taught how to assimilate. Yet, in both contexts, youth was a problem, although one that required different solutions. In both countries, my older Samoan interlocutors expressed a series of shared concerns about Samoan youth: the youth are leaving traditional Samoan churches, don't respect their culture or their parents, don't speak Samoan, and are failing in schools. The youth themselves expressed the mirror image of these concerns, anxious that they were not accepted as Samoan in their parents' communities or in Samoa but are facing prejudice for being Samoan in all other contexts. Generation gaps in both countries were being read as cultural gaps, albeit with different inflections. Parents and older relatives described the youth as potentially acultural, and the youth were routinely frustrated in their attempts to be recognized as Samoan. In general, my interlocutors were all using problems they associated with raising children away from Samoa as a starting point to discuss the consequences of migrating into multiculturalism.

I was not surprised that in New Zealand the most commonly voiced solution to the youth problem was educating the youth about Samoan culture. When I started historical research, I noticed that this argument was also voiced by migrants when they first moved to the United States from Samoa. Even the novice Samoan community workers in the United States would begin their grant applications to various government agencies arguing that Samoan youth need to be taught Samoan culture. Here is a sample quote for a city grant application for funds for a Samoan youth center:

> Much of the virtues and qualities of the Samoan culture remains a mystery due to the youth's limited exposure to their culture with unlike setting they now live in. The revival of these values and traditions in a controlled and adaptable setting will bring about the reverence and respectful nature of their culture. These qualities of life need to be taught and instilled into the youths of today (especially away from their homeland) as a means of self identification rather than the criminal and destructive alternatives.

This grant application, and similar ones espousing Samoan culture, was not funded. As community workers, and Samoan migrants in general, became more experienced with the U.S. context, they stopped arguing for the importance of teaching Samoan youth their culture. In this chapter, I focus on how, in the United States, Samoan community workers began to argue that solving the problems of migrant youth primarily entailed educating the parents.

The dilemmas my interlocutors faced are ones that many migrants face (Hall 2002; Lowe 1996; Ong 2003; Radhakrishnan 1994; Raj 2003). Yet particular cultural assumptions shaped Samoan communities' responses to these common dilemmas. In this chapter, I address how an assimilationist rhetoric can provide Samoan migrants with solutions for problems that emerge from the way Samoan migrant communities in the United States frame their relationship to cultural knowledge. This chapter is divided into three parts: (1) the epistemological assumptions that Samoan migrants often hold; (2) the explanations these Samoan migrants employ to understand their U.S.–raised youth's behavior; and (3) the types of solutions people, especially Samoan community workers, advocate for what they perceive to be a generation gap caused by migration.

This chapter's analysis is based on ethnographic research in nonprofit organizations staffed by people originally from American Samoa. I spent 1998 in San Francisco, conducting research among three Samoan community-based organizations that were primarily funded by various branches of the city government, including the Department of Human Resources, the Mayor's Office of Children, Youth, and Their Families, and the Juvenile Probation Department. Their clients were from both independent and American Samoa, although my survey of four hundred case files indicates that, in cases where this information was available, 32 percent were born in the United States, and 43 percent were born in American Samoa. The rest were born in independent Samoa or didn't provide this information.

Analyses of U.S. integration have largely focused on its relative success, asking "How are migrants adjusting?" By doing so, scholars have focused on strategies people develop to move between two cultures (Alba and Nee 2003; Hall 2004; Portes and Zhou 1993). In this chapter, I am inverting this perspective, asking how migrants invoke the rhetoric of assimilation in response to conceptual possibilities created by migration. Rather than adopting the assumptions underlying the concept of assimilation, I am exploring what uses are served by this concept when my interlocutors in the field invoke it. My interlocutors in the United States uniformly described life after migration as one filled with choices they never had in Samoa. After migration, they explained that they were confronted with the possibility that behaving like a Samoan can be a self-conscious choice. As I discussed in chapter 3, this is antithetical to a Samoan perspective on how cultural identity is formed. In a sense, my interlocutors were explaining to me that migration opened the door to a new perspective on what a person's relationship to social order could be (see Parnell 2000 and Demian 2006 for discussions of comparable transformations). The people I spoke with saw this new and self-conscious relationship to social order in general, and Samoan social order in particular, as a solution to problems Samoan communities were having with the U.S.–raised youth.

The result is that Samoan community workers in the United States will recommend to clients a version of assimilation as a solution for various problems. In the United States, community workers told me that Samoan parents needed to realize that their children had more choices now; that the traditional Samoan parenting techniques do not work in this new context. They encourage parents to change their ways, while simultaneously trying to teach the youth to be more tolerant of their parents' traditional leanings. The Samoan community workers' unexpected lessons of how cultural identity and choice can be intertwined are being taught at the same time as local and national governments are advocating that citizens adopt neoliberal and market-based concepts of agency. Yet the Samoan community workers are espousing a position more complex and culturally resonant than simply a neoliberal perspective.[1] Here I explain why Samoan community workers in the United States will evoke a culturally specific assimilationist rhetoric as one avenue for exploring new relationships to social order and resolving a supposedly new tension between viewing Samoan cultural identity as a choice and as a given.

First, a caveat: only a simplified narrative of the migration process enables generation gaps to become dilemmas that compel migrants to conceptualize assimilation as a possibility, and a possibility that threatens cultural identity. In practice, generations—particularly generations of migrants—are not rigidly segregated without a considerable labor of division

---

1. See Ong (2003) for ethnographic examples in which social workers' practices emerge seamlessly out of neoliberal ideology.

constructing the boundaries between first-generation, second-generation, and third-generation migrants. In any Samoan migrant community, there will be many people of the same age, each with a different life trajectory in relationship to Samoa. Some were born in New Zealand or the United States and never set foot in Samoa. Some will choose to move to Samoa as adults, and then will return to New Zealand or the United States only for retirement. Others misbehaved as teenagers and were sent back to Samoa for a number of years to learn discipline. Some have gone back to Samoa every year for a month or so to live in a parent's village. Still others have just arrived in New Zealand or the United States, and will return to Samoa in a couple of years. In short, migrants circulate between New Zealand, the United States, and Samoa, and therefore generational divides are not illuminating ways to classify people. Regardless of its accuracy, Samoans I spoke to saw generational divisions as useful labels for understanding other Samoans' behavior. This chapter also addresses how Samoan cultural identity is structured so as to make these generational labels compelling enough.

Who Is Samoan?

In one of the Samoan churches I attended, a man in his mid-twenties who also regularly helped with the sound system in church, had been raised in Apia (the capital and largest city in Samoa), spoke colloquial Samoan fluently, but wasn't himself Samoan by blood. People in the church thought of him as being part-Samoan, although the man explained that this wasn't the case when I asked him about it. One woman I spoke with, having been told he wasn't part-Samoan, forgot that conversation two weeks later and explained to me that he was an *afakasi* (literally half-caste, of mixed parentage). He was an anomaly, incongruous enough to require people to forget repeatedly that he knew how to act like a Samoan only because he was raised as one. Samoan migrant concerns about who counts as Samoan are shaped by their epistemological assumptions about being Samoan.

My interlocutors tend to see people's ability to perform social roles properly as rooted in inherited knowledge.[2] Being born Samoan implies

---

2. See Marcus 1991 and 1993 for a comparable discussion of Tongan relationships to roles.

that one knows how to act as a Samoan. In Samoa, supposedly this assumption seems perfectly warranted, especially since learning to be Samoan is often accomplished tacitly within Samoan villages (see Ochs 1988; St. Christian 1994). This is much more difficult to accomplish after migration. In addition, the arenas in which people demonstrate their Samoan cultural expertise has shifted somewhat upon migration, and *fa'alavelave* have become centrally important. In short, Samoan assumptions about how one knows correct Samoan behavior are undermined upon migration, ensuring that Samoan anxieties about assimilation revolve around family members raised outside of Samoa knowing how to behave properly.

What do Samoan youth raised in the United States tend *not* to know about being Samoan? The gaps and omissions that I noticed were different from the ones that Samoan parents complained about to me and others.[3] I noticed both in New Zealand and in the United States that none of my interlocutors raised outside of Samoa distinguished between the two kinds of Samoan chiefs, *ali'i* (high chiefs) and *tulafale* (talking chiefs) or knew about the *feagaiga* (discussed in chapter 4). I once tried to explain the *feagaiga* with little success at a picnic. One U.S.–raised woman kept insisting to me that of course brothers and sisters shared clothes back in Samoa, while her Samoan-raised mother watched bemused and finally disagreed, reminiscing about how careful she was with her cross-sex cousins never to share T-shirts.

What my older interlocutors were concerned that U.S.-raised youth did not know was a slightly different range of cultural knowledge. They were concerned that the youth did not understand the importance of *fa'alavelave* and might stop participating in these costly exchanges when they got older; that the youth did not know how to behave respectfully to their elders, and thus potentially bringing shame on the family; and that the youth did not know the nuances of having a particular Samoan social role, such as how to be a dutiful daughter-in-law, and thus might behave improperly (and disrespectfully). In short, people often saw a tight coupling between being born Samoan and acting like a Samoan, and were uncomfortable or critical when this assumed link was undermined.

---

3. An exception to this is university students who take courses on Pacific ethnography.

Migrating Knowledges

Samoan epistemological assumptions about someone's relationship to cultural knowledge can lead to highly charged situations in migration, especially since children often do not know how to behave properly. In the moment of performance, Samoans do not distinguish between people and their roles, or attend to the labor that goes into learning how to perform a role properly. Elinor Ochs has traced this pattern in her work on language socialization in independent Samoa. She claims that in speech situations, Samoan children are responsible for speaking intelligibly: "Samoan caregivers expect small children to assume most of the burden of making an unintelligible utterance intelligible, and...this practice is tied to expectations concerning social rank, i.e. that a sociocentric demeanor is expected of lower- to higher-ranking persons" (Ochs 1988, 28). From an early stage, the onus of proper behavior resides with the children. When the children do not speak properly, they are publicly teased. "Samoan care givers rely on teasing and shaming to get a clearer utterance from a child. Children who speak unclearly are referred to in their presence as having *guku Saiga* (or *gutu Saina*) 'Chinese mouth' or may be said to talk like a horse or may be called by the name of an adult who doesn't speak or act normally" (Ochs 1988, 134). Ochs here points to the ways in which the labor of language learning is overlooked and linguistic competence is presumed when Samoan caregivers engage with children.

I noticed instances in which roles were seen as natural rather than learned in many different contexts. One incident occurred at the National Office of Samoan Affairs in San Francisco, which housed a community school designed for Samoan youths at risk of failing out of the U.S. public school system (discussed in chapter 3). A top administrator from the city schools was planning to visit, and the coordinator of the Samoan school, Alofa, was discussing with me her plans to welcome this administrator properly. She wanted the students to present a Samoan dance routine to entertain and impress the administrator with the students' cultural abilities. I pointed out that the administrator would be coming in less than a week, and the students wouldn't have time to rehearse. She reassured me that the students didn't need time to rehearse—they were Samoan and would quickly learn any dance. This did not turn out to be the case, and Alofa instead decided to have a handful of the students testify to the supervisor how important the school was to them. Three boys spoke, one after the other, standing at a long, narrow table in front of the administrator, describing how much they appreciated the school. Alofa had substituted oratory for dance at the last minute; oratory, after all, is also a crucial skill in demonstrating one's Samoan cultural knowledge. In general, Alofa's expectations of skills in cultural performance were commonly voiced, and, in my ethnographic work, Samoan elders' expectations of youth's cultural knowledge tended to be more hopeful than realistic.

The Samoan assumption that people are aware of all the social implications of occupying their particular social role can create problems in migration where youth often cannot observe a wide range of Samoan role models. Yet not to act according to one's social role, from a Samoan perspective, is invariably intentional. Other Samoans' interpretive task becomes unraveling the meaning of the omission. Because Samoans are proceeding according to a detailed map of role expectations, they have guidelines for understanding when a silence is an intentional omission, for grasping which of the subtle implicit absences are to be read as strategic. This leaves little space for assuming carelessness or accidental ignorance. Yet New Zealand–and U.S.–raised Samoans often perceive their own mistakes as the result of an innocent ignorance. They are perplexed when others interpret their errors as intentional. The problem for U.S.–raised Samoans is that they are born to be Samoan but do not always know how to behave appropriately in Samoan contexts. My interlocutors believed that this dilemma—of being subject to expectations they lacked the knowledge to fulfill—did not exist in Samoa and was a direct result of the changes in child rearing brought about by migration.

This new dilemma underpins the most common criticisms faced by people raised outside of Samoa. When I was idly chatting with people while doing fieldwork, I attended to the terms they used to judge others' actions. After all, in the process of criticizing, people reveal the types of behavior that not only irritate, but are widely understood to irritate. The two terms my interlocutors most frequently used, both to judge others and to report on others' disapproval of them, were *fia-poto* (to try or want to be smart) and *fia-palagi* (to try or want to be white). Since I had recently left an academic setting, I initially thought *fia-poto* would have positive connotation. Given that my interlocutors in the field described how important it was to act mindful of Samoan cultural knowledge, why was displaying knowledge in this manner disapproved of?

I began to unravel some of the assumptions underlying this charge while talking to a Samoan friend about Michael, a Samoan man who seemed to make many social blunders as the head of a community organization. Michael told me that he tried to be very straightforward. Other people working at the organization, both those employing Michael and those employed by him, seemed bothered because of this straightforwardness. They seemed aggrieved that he was not engaging with them in their particular roles as trustees or employees. So, when talking to my friend who was on the board of trustees for this organization, I would explain Michael's transparently ineffective strategies as products of his lack of political savvy. This did not sit well with my friend, who thought he was *fia-poto*. At this interjection, I shifted tactics and said that I didn't understand others' explanations of his actions. Either they characterized him as too arrogant (an assumption implicit in the *fia-poto* denunciation) or too inept and unaware. It seemed strange to me, I continued, that these were the two options. For me, arrogance and incompetence are not antithetical. My friend shook his head empathetically, and told me that they weren't contradictory for Samoans either. In fact, one implied the other. My friend explained the problem with Michael was that he was too arrogant to recognize his own shortcomings. He was refusing to be properly strategic with other Samoans, and was, in the process, insulting them.

Two tenets help explain why being *fia-poto* is a habitual criticism from the Samoan perspective. First, cultural knowledge exists as a canon, a totality that a person could theoretically know. In general, to be Samoan is to inherently know appropriate behavior in any context defined as Samoan. To fail to behave properly is to undercut the assertion implicit in the act of speaking, that of being Samoan. Second, as I mentioned before, for Samoans, failure is typically seen as intentional. To attempt to do something publicly and not to succeed, or to appear to be in a particular role but not to enact it—this is nonsensical from a Samoan perspective. This is true for many roles; the point is never how well-intentioned someone might be. Either they succeed or they don't.

Accusing someone of being *fia-poto* is the product of juxtaposing these two assumptions. To be *fia-poto* is not to be smart, but to try to be smart. My interlocutors are criticizing the effort of trying to transform what they hold to be an essence—a substance one either has or does not—and making this essence into a state of becoming. Those raised outside of Samoa are constantly being criticized for revealing the effort they put into trying to become something that they should just *be*.

A similar complaint underlies the accusation that someone is *fia-palagi* (trying to be a white person). In these instances, *fia-palagi* criticizes a double failure. First, the term accuses people of denying their family, their origins, and their true identity. In a sense, the term with its critical overtones attacks any perceived attempt at assimilation. But the inevitable failure of this attempted assimilation lurks as a second form of failure within the accusation. A Samoan can never fully be a *palagi,* just as a *palagi* can never be a Samoan. So when a Samoan is being *fia-palagi,* they are failing both to be properly Samoan and to be *palagi*.[4] In all the cases where I heard people using the term *fia-palagi,* there was an implicit criticism of someone's apparently assimilationist tendencies.

At the same time, the term *fia-palagi* contains, from a Samoan perspective, a central paradox that occurs only after migration. The phrase offers

---

4. Samoans in the United States and New Zealand used the term *Fobs* (fresh off the boat; or, less frequently, *freshies*) to criticize newly migrated Samoans. I was captivated by the term *Fob* as a criticism because it initially seemed contradictory to me. My interlocutors raised outside of Samoa would be explaining to me how much they valued being Samoan and how important this was for them as an identity. They might then start describing situations in which they felt as though they possessed less than adequate cultural knowledge to understand how to behave properly or speak properly in a given Samoan context. As the conversation gradually shifted to talking about others, these same people would use the term *Fob* pejoratively (although, if talking about a family member, with a certain amount of affection). Acting like a Fob, or being fobby, is not an accusation reserved only for recent migrants (or even Samoan-born). It can refer to any behavior in a *palagi* context in which the person acted according to Samoan assumptions or principles, and thus acted inappropriately or appeared out of place. I would be puzzled: people were telling me how they wished they understood their Samoan culture better and then would criticize as inept and ineffectual the people who had the knowledge they supposedly desired. When I asked a Samoan friend about this, pointing out that this seemed a bit contradictory, she agreed. She said that this had always bothered her, because people who used the term *Fob* were criticizing their own parents and older relatives implicitly, since all their relatives had to learn how to manage when they first migrated. In addition, they were criticizing people who had just arrived from Samoa and didn't know any better. My friend also revealed that sometimes her friends would tell her how "fobby" she was, largely because of the way she dressed (such as wearing hot pink pig-shaped bedroom slippers when she went shopping). Intriguingly, both those raised outside of Samoa and Samoan-raised share a common assumption when they criticize someone for being a *Fob* or *fia-palagi*—each group is criticizing someone's failure to conform to contextual expectations of appropriate behavior.

the possibility of cultural choice, implying that someone can choose not to be a Samoan or to be acultural. This offers a new way of imagining cultural identity: no longer is one's behavior largely unfolding the possibilities offered by inheritance. The term criticizes people who are denying a cultural identity based on birth but also acknowledges that wanting to choose one's own cultural identity can be a powerful motivating force.

Choosing Culture

On March 3, 1998, a U.S.–raised Samoan with access to the Internet posted the following message on the Polynesian Café (www.polycafe.com):

> For so long it has puzzled me a great deal, finding the right balance between cultural and non-cultural matters. Specifically speaking of my parents, they are very *Fa'a Samoa* [following Samoan culture]. I have discovered in my life that the difficulty of balancing matters between my parents and my own life will remain to be a struggle.... After much discussion with a friend who is going through the same experiences I am, we've resorted to admitting and accepting the fact that this is the way it will always be.

This message encapsulates a central conflict that migrants experience in multicultural nation-states such as the United States: how to balance assumptions that one is born with an identity with the belief that one can choose against one's identity by assimilating, in this case moving away from culture. This writer was expressing familiar migrant anxieties about how cultural identity is constituted, yet the Samoan context she refers to shapes what the struggle between *fa'asamoa* (the Samoan way, embodied by her parents) and her life might be. As I have discussed, being Samoan is fraught with culturally specific dilemmas, many revolving around how people envision the ways to embody Samoan cultural knowledge. The tension between parental demands and children's choices that this migrant mentions is a product of a new conflict created by migration. As a consequence, migrants express anxieties about assimilation that have specifically Samoan nuances, encapsulating dilemmas peculiar to how migration affects Samoan patterns of knowledge transmission.

Samoan migrant parents face a new type of role failure created by migration: children who are born Samoan but do not know how to speak or behave in ways that a Samoan perspective demands. There are a number of ways in which U.S.–raised youth seem to be disrespectful in public Samoan contexts; for example, they do not say *"tulou"* [pardon me] as they walk between two people chatting or crouch a bit when talking to a church minister or older relative to make sure they are not higher than the person in authority. These types of failure are particularly puzzling for Samoans, who tend to see social behavior as an inherited knowledge that people strategically reveal in the appropriate context. This raises the question that haunts Samoan migrant communities: Why don't children raised outside of Samoa know better? Not surprisingly, the explanations my interlocutors offer differ depending on whether people are Samoan-raised or U.S.–raised. Many U.S.–raised youth have told me, "If only my parents would teach me, I would know what to do." The youth wanted explicit instructions, similar to what they are told to expect in U.S. school contexts. As Elinor Ochs (1988) and Alison Jones (1991) have pointed out, teaching rarely occurs in Samoan contexts through explicit instruction. Instead, observation is far more common. Meanwhile, Samoan-raised migrants will tend to talk about parental inattention (when describing other Samoan families), or, in their own cases, they will blame their children's friends. From both perspectives, what could be seen as a gap between being Samoan-raised and U.S.–raised—a migration gap—is being interpreted as a generational gap between parent and child.

I was told some commonly used explanations for a generational divide both in the United States and New Zealand. In each country, my interlocutors would lament the loss of grandparents' input in raising children (see Tanielu 2000, 54). They also discussed Samoan parents' ambivalence about contributing money to *fa'alavelave* and other elements of being Samoan in practice. Parents wanted their children to have new opportunities and be successful in this new country, and contributing to *fa'alavelave* might detract from the children's future. At the same time, parents would be angry when their children erred in Samoan contexts and would scold them publicly. My interlocutors in both countries described these double binds as reasons for the divide.

There were three explanations of children's disobedience and disrespectful behavior that I primarily collected in the United States, and did not hear in New Zealand. First, Samoans in the United States discussed other families' failure to control their children in terms of a lack of supervision. Parents told me that in Samoa there was always someone around to watch children. Even if the parents went to work in the plantations, there would be an aunt or uncle who could supervise them. In the United States, this constant supervision is absent. Samoan migrants would tell me that in the United States parents have to work two jobs to survive, or else they work during the day and play bingo at night. In this sense, my interlocutors are blaming children's poor behavior (which ranged from using disrespectful language to stealing and belonging to a gang) on the lack of an extended family. But they are also blaming children's failure on the ways in which parents are failing to fulfill their Samoan roles.

The second explanation Samoans offered is that the children have friends who lead them astray. This explanation invariably came up when discussing gang membership but was not limited to this context. To a large extent, this is connected to the complaint about the lack of supervision. After all, sufficient parental attention would also entail learning and regulating the children's friends. This explanation is ironic in that part of Samoan knowledge transmission patterns, as Ochs (1988) details,[5] is that children learn much of their information from their age mates. In essence, the parents are complaining that the paths through which children become good and knowledgeable Samoans have, after migration, become precisely the avenues through which these children learn to be disobedient.

The third explanation for children's disobedience and disrespectful behavior is that the U.S. government has begun to intervene in Samoan families in destructive ways, preventing parents from disciplining their children properly. Because discipline is an important component of how Samoan children are expected to learn, this government intervention is perceived as harmful to families. My first indication that child discipline

---

5. Elinor Ochs describes how child-care responsibilities are often distributed among a wide range of caregivers, but placed heavily on older siblings. Adults will monitor children's play, but from a distance. "When the infant is several months old, he or she is left for periods of time with one or more siblings. These older siblings may bring their charges with them to other activities in the village, for example to watch a game or to visit with friends. At four or five in the afternoon, the village is dotted with groups of children holding their younger sibs on their laps or straddled on their hips" (Ochs 1988, 80). A great deal of children's interaction, and hence knowledge transmission, occurs between age mates and older siblings.

was a highly charged topic for Samoan migrants was the response of some Samoans in California to my brief explanation of my research topic. When I introduced myself, I explained that I was studying how government policies impact Samoan families. This frequently elicited stories about government interventions that Samoans felt profoundly disrupted the lines of authority in a family, accounts that invariably revolved around parents' rights to discipline. My project description prompted stories about parents who could no longer discipline their children properly because of the threat of government intervention. One woman told me that her six-year-old daughter had started telling her: "You can't hit me. I know how to dial 9-1-1." These stories would often involve episodes of heroic resistance in which Samoan parents would refuse to allow government officials to curtail their right to teach their children to behave properly. They would make public stands—like spanking their children with a belt in front of the school—to demonstrate their rejection of governmental authority. In these narrations of resistance, Samoan parents were also refusing to accept the way in which the modern nation-state insists that family and government are distinct and colliding entities (see Donzelot 1979).

These were stories that took disciplining children as a productive site for articulating what is Samoan about a family. Discipline is a new arena for forging identity; both the Samoan migrants I interviewed and ethnographers of Samoan childhood attest to this (Duranti 1995; St. Christian 1994). I am not suggesting that discipline becomes a vehicle for teaching children how to be members of a group only after migration, far from that. Rather, Samoans in the United States start discussing discipline as a way to teach children proper *Samoan* behavior, while prior to migration, children were only being taught proper behavior. Douglass-St. Christian, in his dissertation on embodiment in Samoa, describes the lessons discipline is supposed to teach in Western Samoa.

> A punished person is almost immediately reintegrated into his or her family and community following a beating or other punishment. The act of punishment, *fa'a sala,* is the path from a mistake, the ending of an error, and the direction an offender takes back toward communal participation. The physical act of punishment does not avenge the offense, it reminds the offender of the way out of the mistake and back into complete and responsible sociality. (St. Christian 1994, 190)

According to St. Christian, Samoans see discipline as teaching proper sociality, how people should best exhibit their respect and commitment to their families and their villages. However, these communities and families are not defined in terms of cultural difference, as they have been in the Samoan diaspora. Upon migration to the United States, disciplining children becomes laden with anxieties about remaining Samoan in the face of U.S. government attempts to define how families should behave.

Assimilation and Samoan Community Workers

I have been discussing the epistemological assumptions and explanations Samoan migrants evoke as they discuss some specifically Samoan problems of negotiating different cultures. I have been arguing in general terms that Samoan migrants have begun uneasily to think of cultural identity as an identity that can be chosen. This idea of choice is at odds with other assumptions Samoans have about identity as inherited. In this section, I examine a site where this tension is explicitly addressed: when Samoan community workers try to help parents transform their child rearing practices in response to the pressures of living in the United States. Samoan community workers begin to offer a Samoan version of assimilation as a solution to the dilemma migrant parents now face—of thinking of culture simultaneously as a given and as chosen.

In 1998, the U.S. government was in the early stages of implementing the welfare reforms signed into law by President Clinton in 1996 as part of the Personal Responsibility and Work Opportunity Reconciliation Act. This was the first year that people on the welfare rolls faced the two-year limit. As a result, I attended many information sessions in which city government officials tried to explain their strategies for encouraging clients to cooperate with the new "welfare to work" policies. Yet, while both government agencies and Samoan families were expressing considerable anxieties about families' access to resources, the Samoan community organizations were focused largely on addressing the concerns of Samoan youth. Previously the organizations I observed had offered job training and computer training to Samoan communities. The organizations had also been involved in distributing food and organizing older Samoan women to weave fine mats for *fa'alavelave.*

By the time I was doing fieldwork, these projects were on the back-burner, and all the organizations' primary focus was on Samoan youth.[6] These community organizations survived year to year largely due to city grants, most of which were available only to assist "at risk" youth. When I asked community workers why they focused on youth primarily, they never mentioned that granting opportunities affected their commitments. Instead, they mentioned how frustrating working with Samoan communities was in general, and said that helping Samoan youth was the only way they felt like they could have a positive effect.

The Samoan community workers[7] become involved in cases involving parents in three possible ways: (1) a Department of Human Services social worker calls the community organization and requests assistance in handling a case; (2) the nonprofit organization's involvement with the Juvenile Probation Department leads them gradually into this involvement; or (3), the most infrequent path, the parents request their assistance. The most common role the community worker is expected to play is teaching Samoan clients what the government expects of them. Samoan community workers are rarely called on to serve as advocates for their clients, although I know of at least one Samoan worker who had a reputation for consistently and aggressively arguing for his clients in court. As a result, Samoan community workers' role in intervening within the family can

---

6. The Office of Samoan Affairs, where I spent the majority of my time, received outside assistance and funding from three sources: (1) Asian/Pacific Island Hotline, (2) the Juvenile Probation Department through its intensive home-based supervision (IHBS) program, and (3) the San Francisco school system. The Samoan Community Development Center was not as youth-oriented, partially because it received a Community Development Block Grant (CDBG) to help Samoan migrants find housing. This organization also was funded by a Mayor's Office of Children, Youth, and Their Families (MOCYF) grant—a grant begun under Mayor Agnos—which also encouraged a focus on youth. Soul'd Out Productions, a third Samoan organization in San Francisco, was a church-based organization whose primary activity was providing youth with extracurricular activities such as sports and Polynesian dance performances. While they were not able to receive city funds during 1998 (partially because Soul'd Out was a religious organization), this organization had regular luaus—a Hawaiian term that Samoans in the United States have adopted for fund-raising events in which they offered the paying audience a Samoan dinner and a student performance consisting of dances inspired by various Pacific Islands.

7. Most of the people who worked at these organizations identified as Samoan. Teachers who taught in the schools for so-called at-risk Samoan youth were the primary exceptions. These community workers had no special training (aside from intermittent, short training workshops offered by various government agencies) and often became involved in the organization through family connections.

be potentially adversarial from the beginning. From the outset, they face a set of problems because community workers and government officials are claiming a form of authority that violates the hierarchical boundaries Samoan families are accustomed to enforcing.

A Foucaultian analysis of Samoan community workers' interactions with their clients would suggest that these community workers are one among many methods for disciplining families and extending state power (see Moffatt 1999). Migrant families in particular are seen as posing a challenge to the orderliness of state-family relations because migrants have not yet internalized the necessary forms of self-regulation. Social workers are faced with the task of teaching them how to be productive citizens that raise equally productive self-regulating citizens. Indeed, this is the conclusion Aihwa Ong reaches in *Buddha Is Hiding,* an ethnographic exploration of Cambodian refugees, another Asian Pacific American minor minority, in the Bay Area. Ong writes: "[I]n daily encounters, poor newcomers like Cambodian refugees were constituted as particular kinds of unworthy subjects who must be taught to become self-reliant, to be accountable for their situation. The processes intended to produce self-disciplining, provident subjects often rely on ethno-racial notions as the basis for discriminating among, assessing, and penalizing welfare clients" (Ong 2003, 124). Ong describes social workers as encouraging neoliberal state ideals of what makes a good citizen. In the process, social workers treat Cambodian parents as continuing to enact cultural traditions that threaten their children. At the same time, the social workers treat the children as rational and autonomous subjects, not cultural beings (Ong 2003, 168–194). For Ong, the social workers embody the state unproblematically.

This was not the case in my fieldwork, which was with a minor minority group that, like Cambodian refugees, were disadvantaged by being linked through the census to "model minority" Asian Americans such as Chinese or Japanese. The Samoan community workers I interviewed and worked with were often ambivalent about the ways in which government agencies were asking them to further government aims with Samoan families. They were even skeptical of the initial assumed divide between Family and Government, which Jacques Donzelot suggests is crucial to the modern labor of division by which the state determines how families and governments will antagonistically collude to fashion disciplined and productive citizens (Donzelot 1979). By delineating Samoan community workers' unease, I am taking issue with a Foucaultian interpretation of how state workers assist in maintaining this divide between Family and Government. I am suggesting instead that Samoan community workers are refiguring both U.S. government and Samoan community expectations when they attempt to intervene in Samoan parent-child relationships. They do so through an assimilationist rhetoric that defines anew what is choice and what is compulsion from both a Samoan or U.S. government perspective. In short, Samoan community workers are attempting, albeit with mixed results, to transform their clients' reflexive understandings of how one engages with social orders into one more compatible with, but not the same as, neoliberal state understandings.

Samoan community workers are caught in a bind because they are frequently hired by San Francisco's Department of Human Services (DHS) to teach their clients the legitimacy of government intervention in culturally appropriate ways. Yet this very act of intervention is antithetical to a proper Samoan relationship between rules and responsibility. Samoans do not tell each other how to discipline their children unless they are in the right hierarchical position within the extended family. In fact, in the Samoan Congregational church I attended, parents or relatives only will discipline children.[8] The community workers are intervening based on an authority granted them through their relationship to government agencies, an authority that their clients might well feel is illegitimate. Migrants do not share some of the basic assumptions that government officials must believe in order to legitimate their intrusion. As a result, Samoan community workers are placed in a unique trap. They must, often against their better judgment, educate their Samoan clients into recognizing the legitimacy of government intervention. Then, they are expected to reframe the situation for their clients. Once they establish the basis for compelling migrants to be a different kind of parent, they must teach the clients to choose freely to discipline their children differently.

In other words, first the Samoan community worker must make their clients acknowledge that they have a problem—that they are raising their children in such a way that DHS can intercede and remove their children from their care. Then they must teach their clients to think of the problem

---

8. This was not the case in the churches I attended in New Zealand. There, any older person was entitled to discipline those who were younger.

as one built into the very structure of the family, which the parents can actively choose to transform if they are determined to do so. Samoan community workers must teach their clients the nation-state's compulsion before they can encourage them to choose to be "healthy."

Samoan community workers are regularly confronted with the problem of mistrust. The community workers and clients would tell me that Samoan community workers are perceived as being unable to keep secrets. Because they are Samoan, they will spread information about the clients' cases throughout various Samoan communities. Their role as community worker working for a nonprofit organization would always be superseded by their connections to their family and their church, an anxiety that was figured as fear of gossip. The clients' concern is focused on internal community dynamics, not the external government perceptions. In other words, the clients are not generally fearful that the government would learn inappropriate information or that Samoans could not be counted on to advocate properly for their Samoan clients in the face of a confusing and complicated bureaucracy. Rather, the clients worry about how Samoan community workers might use the gleaned information to shame the client's family within Samoan circles. The community workers have to figure out strategies for reassuring the Samoan clients that they are trustworthy and will not circulate information that will damage the family's reputation. In San Francisco, one community worker told me that she reassured Samoan families that she personally adhered to a strict division between work and family. For her, the role of a community worker ensured that she would not divulge any information about particular cases.

This reassurance was a first step in teaching Samoan clients about the distinction between government and family, as well as providing them insights into how Samoan community workers positioned themselves in this divide. Samoan case workers must convince their clients that their roles as community workers are distinct from their roles as Samoan community members and that they had internalized this distinction. The community workers, in short, must convince their clients that they are acultural to a certain degree when they are being community workers. But this is a position that is antithetical to how Samoans manage their own relationships to roles. From a Samoan perspective, one's role is the result of a particular context. As I have discussed, people tend not to be able to choose to be particular roles because the context often compels them to adopt a given role.

There are many situations in which the exact role is not readily apparent, when a person is related to another through a variety of relationships, and hence can act according to one of several possible relationships. In these cases, there will be some negotiating to determine which role a person will be for the duration of that context. There is a certain amount of fluidity in these roles, which can create tension. When Samoan community workers claim that their jobs ensure a relationship based on confidentiality, they are denying the contextual and fluid nature of Samoan roles. They are implicitly teaching their clients the first step to recognizing a conceptual division between government and family.

After Samoan social workers have established their trustworthiness by introducing a new vision of how roles structure people's behavior, they have to teach their clients that government agencies have the right to intercede in their family hierarchies. This seems odd to Samoan families. In Samoan families, the person who imposes rules also assumes responsibility for outcomes. Government agencies are imposing both rules and responsibilities in one fell swoop. They require people to take full responsibility for the success or failure of the family as a unit, while proffering the guidelines that will determine this success. When the families fail to conform to the imposed standards, then government officials step in to help. In Samoan families, the same expectations of respect and conformity apply to everyone. It would make no sense to have a division between familial actions and government expectations, with government officials demanding certain practices without the officials themselves also being forced to wrestle these restrictions. While government agencies distinguish between being a community worker and being a mother, the San Francisco Samoan community workers I interviewed reject this distinction. Often their case notes will reflect this tension, describing how "as a mother" they find themselves insisting on parent-child relationships dominated by respect and obedience. The Samoan community workers' quandary is that they must, in the process of helping their clients, teach them this new way of distinguishing family responsibility from state responsibility and thus a new way of attributing agency and responsibility.

An early task of Samoan community workers, after explaining that their role ensures confidentiality, is to remind their clients to exhibit the respect demanded in Samoan hierarchical relations. In other words, the community workers try to reassert a code of behavior that all Samoans are assumed to understand: the need to respect and serve those who are hierarchically superior to you. When speaking to youth, the community workers will often invoke this ideology by attributing motivations such as love to parents' attempts to discipline. The youth are chastised for not respecting their parents and showing this disrespect by not obeying them. Parents are reminded of their duties to their children, the need to care for their children in such a way that the children are expected to obey rules and behave appropriately. A Samoan case worker described one of her sessions between a young, rebellious girl and her two, too lenient parents in which she tried to establish clear hierarchical relationships:

> The girl interrupted me several times while I was trying to explain her problems. Not only was she rude, but she was starting to get very loud. The parents on the other hand just sit there and say nothing. At this time, I told the girl to behave herself, and it is very rude to cut someone in the middle of a statement to raise her objections without waiting her turn. She immediately said that she does that all the time to her parents and they don't care. "Well, I am not your parents and I will not tolerate this kind of behavior." The girl pouted but kept quiet for a while, and the father tried to say something, except I held up my hand and continue with introducing the problem at hand as well as introducing what I am planning to do to try and help the girl with her problems as well as having them as part of this rehab session.

In short, Samoan community workers are invoking Samoan ideological attempts at creating compulsion within people. They are describing the interwoven principles of love, respect, and obedience that are supposed to underpin parent-child relationships. These statements are assertions of ideal Samoan family interactions in the rawest form. Not to adhere to them, at least verbally, is to reject the ways in which parents and children affirm their relationships on a daily basis, and thus, ultimately, to reject the relationship altogether. By reminding the family members about the expectations that frame the Samoan-inflected relationship between parent and child, the Samoan community worker reminds the family of the rules that are supposed to determine their interactions. The community workers are setting the stage for demanding that Samoan families adhere to practices that they are supposed to always already enact as Samoans. The compulsion, in this instance, lies in the expectations underpinning what it means to love a relative as a Samoan.

When Samoan community workers are addressing their clients, they are wielding two types of compulsion. They are teaching the Samoan families that governments can and will intervene within families, that each member is expected to work toward creating a functional family, a functionality that the government defines. In addition, Samoan community workers are evoking Samoan communities' expectations of appropriate behavior. In essence, these two types of compulsion are contradictory because the division between government and family presupposes an allocation of responsibility that Samoan families implicitly reject in their hierarchical structures and tactics of decision making. It is partially to resolve the tension between these two kinds of compulsion lurking in the background that Samoan community workers then stage the next step in placing families on the road to functionality: they help construct choice.

Samoan community workers, faced with the unpleasant burden of evoking two contradictory forms of compulsion in the families they serve, tend to frame the problem in terms of cultural differences. Rather than describing the tensions in terms of family dysfunction, they are prone to describe it as one of the hazards of assimilation. In presenting their clients with reasons to change their behavior, they suggest that formerly effective Samoan parenting techniques no longer work in the United States. While in Samoa, children were obedient and respectful; in the United States, they are corrupted by other children and negative media influences. One community worker I interviewed described a recent counseling session with a Samoan mother whose children had been removed by DHS. She explained the parent training/counseling session in the following terms, having introduced the topic of what each family member should do:

> The client presented only the Samoan culture version, which is a child should only be seen and not heard; a child should do as told and not to ask why; and since the parents knows better, they are the sole decision making in the family. The client is a typical Samoan mother, raised back home in Samoa under the above condition. Based on the way she was brought up, she is absolutely correct. I reminded her that the Samoan way is not of the American ways. There are laws governing the well-being of a child. Although we were brought up to do as told, the roles and structures in the United States are very different, and since we are residing in the United States we must understand and adhere to these rules and regulations if we are to keep our nuclear family together.

The Samoan community worker went on to explain that she will then teach clients (this one included) that there are any number of rules and a continuum of acceptable parenting styles that parents can apply to their offspring, and that Samoan parents will err on the side of strictness. If their children's friends can go to the movies, stay out late, date, and enjoy other freedoms, the children begin to resent their parents' restrictions.

Samoan community workers teach families that the dilemma they confront is one of too many choices. These choices are presented implicitly as criticisms of other cultures' parenting. Samoan disciplining patterns are not in themselves wrong; they are simply less effective when the children see the discipline as a choice (as Americans do) rather than as a necessity.[9] The same logic that allows families to choose to be healthy also encourages children to think of parental restrictions as fundamentally arbitrary. The community workers teach that diversity has ensured that parents can no longer control their children through the techniques that they are accustomed to using and that they must develop new approaches.

Samoan community workers are walking a fine line. They cannot criticize Samoan culture for several reasons. First, their organizations are based on the assumption that Samoan culture offers valid and productive techniques for resolving family dilemmas. Second, such criticism would involve expressing shame about their own identity, a stance it would be extraordinarily difficult for these community workers to take. Third, one of their main techniques for compelling their Samoan clients to change their behavior relies on guidelines expressed in Samoan cultural ideology. At the same time, some of these same explicit principles are creating problems between parents and children in transition.

Intriguingly, the community workers rarely talk about a cultural gap between the Samoan parents and their social or economic settings. Samoan parents often struggle to meet the financial demands of assisting

---

9. While using culture to advocate for new forms of discipline was often a successful explanation for the parents, this was not as effective an explanation for the children. As one case worker told me after a grueling session:

> The boy fails to understand why his father did this to all of them regardless of his upbringing and the culture. If he was going to be that mean, why have them in the first place. He said that his parents are using the culture as an excuse to their own meanness and stupidity. The boy insisted that he is not buying into this culture concept of discipline.

an extended Samoan family as well as supporting a household on a low-income salary. The larger economic pressures are rarely discussed in these parenting sessions. Rather, the cultural gap emerges between Samoan parents and their children, who are understood to be adopting U.S. practices and expectations. The children are often described as too disobedient—asking questions inappropriately, not obeying parents' direct order, choosing unworthy friends, and insisting on dating. Rather than discussing culture with Samoan parents in terms of the larger forces that impinge on their lives, community workers focus only on the presumed cultural gap between parent and child. This became apparent when a case worker was describing her counseling session with a grandmother who is raising her three grandchildren on her own:

> The grandmother admitted that she...finds it very hard to reward Sila [her granddaughter] when doing well. [The grandmother said:] "It is not our nature to do likewise. Sila should know I always love her, and I don't need to show it." That is when I explained to the grandmother that those were the old ways. This is America; it is a different world and there are so many other people that influence Sila's life, and if she continues to ignore Sila in that way and not compliment her for doing well or telling her she loves her, how will Sila know?

Whenever the community workers talked about Samoan forms of discipline, they would describe how these forms are inappropriate in an American context, where the government will be motivated to intervene if Samoan children seem to have been disciplined physically at home too harshly.

Thus, Samoan community workers describe the relationship between parents and children as generation gaps that are becoming refigured as cultural gaps. But for Samoan social workers, it is the influx of influences, not the diffusion of them, that has created the dilemma. For Samoan social workers, too much choice has led to a treacherous cycle in which their clients must be confronted with other compulsions in order to change "traditional" family patterns. Yet in practice, the compulsions implicit in Samoa—ensuring that an extended family and village pressure children into behaving properly—no longer exist. As a result, Samoan parents have become the sole disciplinarians for their children. Discipline was spread out in Samoa as a responsibility belonging to many relatives, but in the United States fewer people are obligated to discipline. Techniques that others used to mitigate discipline (grandparents' intervening, children being sent to live with other relatives), can be far more complicated and difficult to implement in an urban environment. These are only some of the many changes that have affected Samoan disciplining practices after migration, but the Samoan social workers tend to focus on the hazards of presenting other ways of living to Samoan children.

In advocating a tempered form of child discipline, Samoan community workers are attempting to teach Samoan parents to imagine anew the ways in which compulsion and choice are cultural, to rethink their relationship to a social order. From a Samoan perspective, being Samoan means obeying unquestioningly certain cultural compulsions, such as respecting parents and obeying hierarchical superiors without question. Refusal is not read as an expression of freedom but as an insult to one's Samoan family and culture. Thus, choice in the individualistic sense is not to be practiced publicly; from this perspective it is asocial. By explaining children's behavior as a product of U.S. cultural influences, Samoan community workers are trying to convince Samoan parents that individual choice is not only cultural but an integral part of the U.S. experience. At the same time, they are encouraging families to understand compulsion as acultural from a Samoan perspective. After all, Samoan parents are being expected to follow rules established by an abstracted authority, government, one whose representatives accept neither the responsibility nor the shared compulsions that go hand-in-hand with rules in America Samoa. In short, in an attempt to teach Samoan families the American way of distinguishing government from family, Samoan community workers are advocating cultural choices and taking the culture out of compulsion.

When people from Samoa move to the United States, they encounter new possible relationships to social order. For perhaps the first time, they do not have to behave like a Samoan, their cultural identity becomes a choice and not a compulsion. This new possibility is antithetical to the assumptions Samoans employ to interpret each others' behavior and generates common condemnations that some Samoans are *fia-palagi* (trying to be white) and disrespectful. While these are general tensions, the paradoxes become heightened around U.S.–raised Samoans' behavior and, as a consequence, the parent-child relationship. When people consciously attempt to resolve these paradoxes, as in the case of Samoan community workers, they will tend to use an assimilationist rhetoric and focus on the Samoan parents as the locus for potential effective change.

In this chapter, I have turned to a common experience for migrants in general: how raising children in nations other than where the parents were raised can focus attention on the consequences of migrating into multiculturalism. Youth become symbolic tokens as Samoan communities and families debate how best to navigate new contexts. As they participate in this debate, Samoan community workers evoke terms implicating culture and assimilation. In the United States, Samoan community workers insisted that the parents needed to be taught another approach, the American way. In educating parents about the need for a form of assimilation, however, Samoan community workers kept invoking Samoan ideological assumptions, such as the importance of respecting certain hierarchies. Ultimately, Samoan community workers were refiguring how compulsion and choice are supposed to function in social contexts, mixing Samoan cultural assumptions with neoliberal government expectations. This fusion was not at the level of the content of what might count as compulsion or choice. Rather, Samoan community workers were recommending that their clients reflexively fashion a different relationship to cultural orders, one that enabled culture to be a choice.

Samoan community workers create an account of choice and culture that is compatible with neoliberal assumptions about selves as choice makers but not identical with these assumptions. To engage with their clients, Samoan community workers had to fashion a rhetoric of assimilation that acknowledged and legitimated two contradictory ways of carving up the world: both neoliberal and Samoan and neither. In doing so, Samoan community workers counseled a new reflexive relationship to social orders.

In practice, this focus on the generation gap as a cultural gap draws attention away from connections made possible by what C. Wright Mills terms a "sociological imagination" (Mills 1959; see also Eliasoph 1998). The dilemmas between parents and children could be understood as the consequences of larger sociological forces. Yet economic inequalities, bureaucratic racism, or other large-scale factors are all overlooked by the community workers' social analysis as they focus on how to reframe the ways in which culture, and in particular Samoan culture, engenders choice and compulsion. In these instances, an anthropological imagination—a focus on cultural differences and their consequences—was clashing with a sociological imagination—a focus on the connections between the personal and the political.

I have been focusing on how assimilationist explanations can allow people to reconfigure their relationship to social order, particularly a Samoan social order, by offering a self-referential perspective that enables Samoan community workers to portray identity as a choice. In many ways, what I have been describing is not the experience of migration from a Samoan perspective, but one of the ways by which people construct themselves as migrants. In the process, differences between independent Samoa and American Samoa become less salient. By envisioning Samoa as this unified haven, this counterpoint to the United States' unpredictable multiculturalism, Samoan community workers are able to approach a generation gap as a cultural gap. They are not only experimenting with different relationships to social orders, they are positing their clients and themselves as Samoan first and foremost, and as American more grudgingly. Part of the work of constructing choice across the cultural/acultural divide is also constructing what it means to be a migrant.

Conclusion

In New Zealand and the United States, being Samoan means being a culture-bearer. The moment a person who is Samoan starts dealing with government bureaucracies, they enter a system in which some people and practices are understood as acultural, and others are marked as cultural. And Samoans are almost always cultural. Because of the long histories of other dominant minorities' relationships with government officials and government bureaucracies, being a culture-bearer has different implications in New Zealand than it does in the United States. In New Zealand, Māori politicians and activists have helped engineer government contexts in which having a culture entails having culture along recognizably Polynesian lines, and so is familiar for Samoans and other Pacific migrants. The New Zealand government recognizes and supports all sorts of cultural practices that both Māori and Samoans will describe as cultural within their own communities, such as ritual exchanges and elegant oratory. Not so in the United States, where long-standing interactions with African Americans, Latinos, and Asian Americans ensure that ethnic classifications do not map well onto Samoan migrants' ways of being cultural in their own communities. These different definitions of being a culture-bearer affect the kinds of resources available to communities and families, as well as the strategies they develop for dealing with bureaucracies.

This has concrete consequences for Samoan migrants' experiences of social mobility over the past sixty years. Migrants to both countries began arriving in the 1950s during the postwar economic expansion. They tended to find working-class jobs in both countries, working in factories, hospitals, nursing homes, or on the docks. Yet fifty years later, many who migrated to New Zealand have become lawyers, doctors, social workers, television producers, policy analysts, artists, and so on, while Samoans in the United States have not been able to be hired into similar jobs. What accounts for these different rates of social mobility? This book suggests that definitions of culture play a significant role. Both governments, in dialogue with the dominant minorities in each country, define what counts as culture in ways that advantage Samoan migrants in New Zealand and disadvantage Samoan migrants in the United States.

At the same time that Samoan migrants are navigating different government bureaucracies as culture-bearers, they are also navigating changing government bureaucracies. The years I was studying Samoan migrant families (1996–1998) were the same years that these bureaucracies were incorporating neoliberal legislation and principles into their institutional infrastructure. Both New Zealand and U.S. governments were using culture as justification for increasing decentralization and privatization of government services. The community organizations I studied existed precisely because these governments were funding nongovernmental community organizations that could be culturally appropriate to perform some of the family interventions previously relegated to social welfare departments. In the late 1990s, Samoan migrants were also adjusting to the ways in which culture was becoming more and more integral to the skill sets that government bureaucracies imagined their clients possess.

Just as Samoan migrants were adjusting to new ways in which government bureaucracies were valuing culture anew (see Comaroff and Comaroff 2009; Hale 2005), as I wrote and revised this book, scholars were also rethinking the work culture can and should perform as an analytical concept. This book is an intervention in these discussions in two ways. First, I suggest that understanding how the cultural is constructed is not enough.

Scholars must also understand how the acultural is constructed, and, by doing so, they can make visible some of the unique prices that one must pay under neoliberalism in being a culture-bearer. Second, I suggest turning to questions of reflexivity on the ground as a way to continue asking analytical questions about epistemological differences without reinscribing the well-known problems that culture as an analytical concept potentially has (see Abu-Lughod 1991; Brightman 1994; Strathern 1995; Wagner 1981).

Throughout this book, I focus on the ways people were social analysts in their own right, and how their social analysis shaped how they were engaging with what they understood to be culture and what other people understood to be culture. What counts as culture is a constantly moving target. It is constantly moving in part because people bring different understandings and practices to play in fashioning what will count as culture. I have focused on these understandings as contextually specific reflexivity. I define *reflexivity* as the shifting social analysis that is specific to the social order one is committing (or forced) to enact. Reflexivity and its power lies at the heart of the multiple contrasts in this book: between my understanding of the culture concepts and the understanding of my interlocutors in the field, between being cultural and acultural, between the multiple social orders present in certain contexts. By focusing on Samoan migrants' reflexive interactions with different social orders, I have been able to discuss cultural differences and how such differences emerge without assuming that these differences derive from clashing and preexisting worldviews. Focusing on reflexivity also enables analysis of contexts replete with multiple social orders without presuming that there is a one-to-one connection between one's potential for agency and the structures one encounters. Emphasizing reflexivity brings into sharp focus that the different epistemological assumptions underlying how people engage with cultural knowledge shapes the ways in which social relationships can and will unfold in multicultural and multi-acultural contexts.

I have been consistently addressing the reflexive stance people take toward the families and communities to which they belong, exploring the multivalent layers of commitment people have, and are perceived by others as having, to these various social unities. The varying ways in which people discuss their identity often points to their conscious alignment and frequent realignments with families as they circulate knowledge and resources. The Samoan migrants I write about were often implicitly posing the following question: How should Samoanness be both claimed and practiced to be part of a Samoan family? This was a question created by a family's reconfiguring. As knowledge begins to flow along new paths and greater distances, people begin to reflect on these changes. When people discuss their identity, they are also commenting on the ways that families have changed; identity is a useful category for reflecting on these reconfigurations (see Marshall 2004). Thus *identity* in my account is not an achievement or an inherent quality, despite Samoan migrants' claims to the contrary; it is a signpost for the ways that Samoan families constitute their diasporas.

Beginning with reflexivity offers a variety of insights into how differences are made cultural and how boundaries between different social orders are constructed and maintained. In chapter 1, focusing on people's social analysis of situations revealed that people must circulate knowledge in certain ways so as to maintain distinctions between two different exchange systems. Focusing on reflexivity also sheds light on Samoan migrants' experiences of conversion between forms of Christianity. For Samoan migrants, reflexivity constitutes the meaningful difference between older forms and newer forms of Christianity. Converting from one form of Christianity to another was an opportunity to redefine what was considered meaningful and meaningless ways of worshipping, to reimagine the cultural and the acultural by changing one's reflexive understandings of a moral economy.

In the second part of the book, I explored how Samoan migrants' and government officials' reflexive understandings of the divide between the cultural and acultural shaped their interactions. Government officials' beliefs that they operate within a system were at odds with Samoan migrants' understandings that they were part of a culture. This tension between being part of a bureaucratic system or part of Samoan culture was most visible around "cultural mediators." Mediators or translators were roles that government officials required that Samoan communities produce and that Samoan communities tend to find inherently suspect.

Differences in reflexive understandings were also at the heart of the conflicts between Samoan approaches to families and New Zealand legislators' approaches to families and their dysfunctions. New Zealand legislators kept interpreting families in terms of the principles they associated with nuclear families, framing appropriate family dynamics solely in these terms. Samoans, however, were part of extended families whose primary focus was participating in local and transnational exchanges. Samoans thus understood what constituted a functional family in very different terms than New Zealand legislators did. This reflexive understanding underpinned Samoan migrants' frustrated reaction to New Zealand family legislation, despite legislators' efforts to base the legislation on how Māori and Samoan families supposedly resolved family conflicts.

Finally, the last chapter addressed how Samoan community workers tried to transform their clients' reflexive understandings of what it means to have a culture. They sought to teach other Samoan community members that culture in the United States was more optional than it was in Samoa, that in the United States, one could choose what cultural rules one followed. Samoan community workers urged migrant parents to take into account this new milieu of choice when they disciplined their children. Capitalism, Christianity, choice—all become alternatives to Samoan culture as people understand and produce the boundaries between the cultural and the acultural.

By focusing on my interlocutors' reflexive social analysis of their contexts, I learned that certain moments would often be defined as filled with cross-cultural communication by people in my field sites. These were moments when radically different interpretations of intentions were at play and when radically different premises seemed to shape how people were circulating knowledge and resources. In talking about explanations of intentions, I am not suggesting that cultural differences are at play when there are disagreements over whether selfishness or lust is motivating someone. Rather, differences are made cultural when people disagree over how selves can have intentions, or when there are disagreements about what counts as spontaneous behavior and what counts as reactive behavior. For example, differences are made cultural when one person interprets all behavior as a calculated choice while another person analyzes most public performances as displays of traditional culture.

I also identify differences as cultural when people had different expectations of how to circulate knowledge or resources. My Samoan interlocutors viewed one of their central dilemmas in diaspora as the problem of being caught between two economic systems, of having to move resources from a capitalist arena into *fa'alavelave*. In doing so, my interlocutors were expressing a general dilemma of capitalism—whether to prioritize creating value through capital or through social relationships—and framing this as a uniquely Samoan dilemma. They were framing this problem as one of cultural difference, and thus were addressing differences of exchange as cultural. They characterize the differences as existing between acultural economies and Samoan exchanges. In other contexts that my readers might themselves participate in, these dilemmas are not necessarily seen as an issue of cultural difference but of work and family balance. I explore how my interlocutors found strategic ignorance an effective stopgap solution for these dilemmas partially because they were interpreting the distinctions in terms of cultural differences. People's understanding of their relationship to social orders shapes their solutions to perceived problems.

This is a book that suggests some analytical techniques for addressing a commonplace problem: How do people navigate contexts in which multiple social orders exist simultaneously? The contemporary situations Samoan migrants find themselves in strongly influenced what I end up suggesting. They often had to navigate government bureaucracies that operated as putatively acultural systems and that required them to be culture-bearers. Or they had to labor actively to create boundaries between moral economies and exchange systems because it was practically and conceptually impossible to operate in both at the same time. All these techniques are a testament to the creativity and sophistication of people navigating social orders only minimally of their own making.

REFERENCES

Ablon, Joan. 1971a. "The Social Organization of an Urban Samoan Community."
   Southwestern Journal of Anthropology 27(1): 75–96.
——. 1971b. "Bereavement in a Samoan Community." *British Journal of Medical Psy-
   chology* 44(4): 329–337.
Abu-Lughod, Lila. 1991. "Writing against Culture." In *Recapturing Anthropology:
   Working in the Present,* edited by Richard Fox, 137–162. Santa Fe, NM: School of
   American Research Press.
Addo, Ping-Ann. 2009. "Forms of Transnationalism, Forms of Tradition: Cloth and
   Cash as Ritual Exchange Valuables in the Tongan Diaspora." In *Migration and
   Transnationalism: Pacific Perspectives,* edited by Helen Lee and Steve Tupai Francis,
   43–56. Canberra: The Australian National University E Press.
Addo, Ping-Ann, and Niko Besnier. 2004. "When Gifts Become Commodities: Pawn-
   shops, Valuables, and Shame in Tonga and the Tongan Diaspora." *Journal of Royal
   Anthropological Institute* 14: 39–59.
Akin, David, and Joel Robbins, eds. 1999. *Money and Modernity: State and Local Curren-
   cies in Melanesia.* Pittsburgh: University of Pittsburgh Press.
Alba, Richard, and Victor Nee. 2003. *Remaking the American Mainstream: Assimilation
   and Contemporary Immigration.* Cambridge, MA: Harvard University Press.

Alexeyeff, Kalissa. 2004. "Love Food: Exchange and Sustenance in the Cook Islands Diaspora." *Australian Journal of Anthropology* 15(1): 68–79.

Anae, Melani. 1998. *Fofoaivaoese: The Identity Journeys of New Zealand-Born Samoans.* PhD diss., University of Auckland.

———. 2001. "The New 'Vikings of the Sunrise': New Zealand-Borns in the Information Age." In *Tangata O Te Moana Nui: The Evolving Identities of Pacific Peoples in Aotearoa/New Zealand,* edited by Cluny Macpherson, Paul Spoonley, and Melani Anae, 101–121. Palmerston North: Dunmore Press.

Appadurai, Arjun. 1986. "Theory in Anthropology: Center and Periphery." *Comparative Studies in Society and History* 28(2): 356–361.

———. 1996. *Modernity at Large: Cultural Dimensions of Globalization.* Minneapolis: University of Minnesota Press.

Asang, Isebong. 1999. "Remaking Footprints: Palauan Migrants in Hawaii." *The Contemporary Pacific* 12(2): 371–384.

Asian Pacific Islander American Health Forum (APIAHF). 2004. "Diverse Communities, Diverse Experiences: The Status of Asian Americans & Pacific Islanders in the U.S. San Francisco, CA." http://www.aapcho.dreamhosters.com/download/PDF/Diverse%20Communities%20Diverse%20Experiences.pdf.

Axel, Brian. 2004. "The Context of Diaspora." *Cultural Anthropology* 19(1): 26–60.

Baily, Samuel. 1969. "Italians and the Development of Organized Labor in Argentina, Brazil, and the United States, 1880–1914." *Journal of Social History* 3: 123–134.

Ballard, Chris. 2000. "The Fire Next Time: The Conversion of the Huli Apocalypse." *Ethnohistory* 47(1): 205–225.

Barker, John, ed. 1990. *Christianity in Oceania: Ethnographic Perspectives.* Lanham, MD: University Press of America.

Barker, John. 2001. "Recent Change in Pacific Island Christianity" / "Les mutations récentes du christianisme en Océanie." *New Pacific Review / La Nouvelle Revue du Pacifique* 1(1): 108–117.

Benhabib, Selya. 2002. *The Claims of Culture: Equality and Diversity in the Global Era.* Princeton, NJ: Princeton University Press.

Benjamin, Walter. 1968. "The Task of the Translator." In *Illuminations,* translated by Harry Zohn, 69–82. New York: Harcourt, Brace and World.

Bercovitch, Eytan. 1994. The Agent in the Gift: Hidden Exchange in Inner New Guinea. *Cultural Anthropology* 9(4): 498–536.

Besnier, Niko. 2004. "Consumption and Cosmopolitanism: Practicing Modernity at the Second-Hand Marketplace in Nuku'alofa, Tonga." *Anthropological Quarterly* 77(1): 7–45.

———. 2011. *On the Edge of the Global: Modern Anxieties in the Pacific Island Nation.* Stanford, CA: Stanford University Press.

Bohannon, Paul. 1959. "The Impact of Money on an African Subsistence Economy." *Journal of Economic History* 19: 491–503.

Bourdieu, Pierre. 1977. *Outline of a Theory of Practice.* Translated by Richard Nice. Cambridge: Cambridge University Press.

———. 1984. *Distinction: A Social Critique of the Judgement of Taste.* Translated by Richard Nice. Cambridge, MA: Harvard University Press.

Bowker, Geoffrey, and Susan Leigh Star. 1999. *Sorting Things Out: Classification and Its Consequences.* Cambridge, MA: MIT Press.

Boyer, Dominic. In press. Reflexivity Reloaded: From Anthropology of Intellectuals to Critique of Method to Studying Sideways. http://rice.academia.edu/DominicBoyer/Papers/392642/Reflexivity_Reloaded.

Bozic-Vrbancic, S. 2003. "One Nation, Two Peoples, Many Cultures: Exhibiting Identity at Te Papa Tongarewa." *Journal of the Polynesian Society* 112(3): 295–313.

Brettell, Caroline B., ed. 1993. *When They Read What We Write: The Politics of Ethnography.* Westport, CT: Bergin and Garvey.

———. 2003. *Anthropology and Migration: Essays on Transnationalism, Ethnicity, and Identity.* Walnut Creek, CA: Altamira Press.

Briggs, Charles L. 2001. "Modernity, Cultural Reasoning, and the Institutionalization of Social Inequality: Racializing Death in a Venezuelan Cholera Epidemic." *Comparative Studies in Society and History* 43(4): 665–700.

Brightman, Robert. 1995. "Forget Culture: Replacement, Transcendence, Relexification." *Cultural Anthropology* 10(4): 509–546.

Brodkin, Karen. 1998. *How Jews Became White Folks: And What That Says About Race in America.* Piscataway, NJ: Rutgers University Press.

Brown, Richard. 1995. "Hidden Foreign Exchange Flows: Estimating Unofficial Remittances to Tonga and Western Samoa." *Asian and Pacific Migration Journal* 4(1): 35–54.

Brown, Wendy. 2006. American Nightmare: Neoliberalism, Neoconservativism, and De-Democratization. *Political Theory* 34(6): 690–714.

Buck, Peter (Te Rangi Hīroa). 1930. *Samoan Material Culture.* Honolulu: Bernice P. Bishop Museum.

Calkins, Faye G. 1971. *My Samoan Chief.* Honolulu: University of Hawai`i Press.

Cavell, Stanley. 1984. *Themes out of School: Effects and Causes.* San Francisco: North Point Press.

Chappell, David A. 1999. "Transnationalism in Central Oceanian Politics: A Dialectic of Diasporas and Nationhood?" *Journal of the Polynesian Society* 108(3): 277–304.

Chock, Phyllis Pease. 1999. "'A Very Bright Line': Kinship and Nationality in the U.S. Congressional Hearings on Immigration." *PoLAR: Political and Legal Anthropology Review* 22(2): 42–52.

Chua, Liana. 2009. "To Know or Not to Know? Practices of Knowledge and Ignorance among Bidayuhs in an 'Impurely' Christian World." *Journal of Royal Anthropological Institute* 15(2): 332–348.

Clifford, James. 2001. "Indigenous Articulations." *The Contemporary Pacific* 13(2): 467–490.

Coles, Kimberly. 2007. *Democratic Designs: International Intervention and Electoral Practices in Postwar Bosnia-Herzegovina.* Ann Arbor: University of Michigan Press.

Connell, John, and Richard P. C. Brown. 1995. "Migration and Remittances in the South Pacific: Towards New Perspectives." *Asian and Pacific Migration Journal* 4(1): 1–33.

Comaroff, John L., and Jean Comaroff. 2009. *Ethnicity, Inc.* Chicago: University of Chicago Press.

Coombe, Rosemary. 2011. "'Possessing Culture': Political Economies of Community Subjects and Cultural Rights." In *Ownership and Appropriation,* edited by Veronica Strang and Mark Busse, 105–130. Oxford: Berg.

Crapanzano, Vincent. 1994. "Kevin: On the Transfer of Emotions." *American Anthropologist.* 96(4): 866–885.

Cruikshank, Barbara. 1999. *The Will to Empower: Democratic Citizens and Other Subjects.* Ithaca, NY: Cornell University Press.

Demian, Melissa. 2006. "Reflecting on Loss in Papua New Guinea." *Ethnos* 71(4): 507–532.

Diaz, Vicente. 2004. "To 'P' or Not to 'P'?": Marking the Territory Between Pacific Islander and Asian American Studies." *Journal of Asian American Studies* 7(3): 183–208.

Diaz, Vicente, and J. Kehaulanui Kauanui, eds. 2000. "Native Pacific Cultural Studies on the Edge." Special issue, *The Contemporary Pacific* 13(2): 315–342.

Donzelot, Jacques. 1979. *The Policing of Families.* Translated by Robert Hurley. New York: Pantheon Books.

Drozdow-St. Christian, Douglass. 2002. *Elusive Fragments: Making Power, Propriety and Health In Samoa.* Durham, NC: Carolina Academic Press.

Duranti, Alessandro. 1984. "Intentions, Self, and Local Theories of Meaning: Words and Social Action in a Samoan Context." Center for Human Information Processing report no. 122. La Jolla: University of California, San Diego. http://www.sscnet. ucla.edu/anthro/faculty/duranti/reprints/intsel.pdf.

———. 1993. "Intentions, Self, and Responsibility: An Essay in Samoan Ethnopragmatics." In *Responsibility and Evidence in Oral Discourse,* edited by Jane Hill and Judith Irvine, 24–47. Cambridge: Cambridge University Press.

———. 1994. *From Grammar to Politics: Linguistic Anthropology in a Western Samoan Village.* Berkeley: University of California Press.

———. 1995. "Indexical Speech across Samoan Communities." *American Anthropologist* 99(2): 342–354.

Dureau, Christine. 1998. "Decreed Affinities: Nationhood and the Western Solomon Islands." *Journal of Pacific History* 33(2): 197–220.

Dusenbery, Verne. 1997. "The Poetics and Politics of Recognition: Diasporan Sikhs in Pluralist Polities." *American Ethnologist* 24(4): 738–762.

Eliasoph, Nina. 1998. *Avoiding Politics: How Americans Produce Apathy in Their Everyday Lives.* Cambridge: Cambridge University Press.

Elliston, Deborah. 1998. "Geographies of Gender and Politics: The Place of Difference in Polynesian Nationalism." *Cultural Anthropology* 15(2): 171–216.

Epstein, A. L. 1969. "The Network and Urban Social Organization." In *Social Networks in Urban Situations: Analyses of Personal Relationships in Central African Towns,* edited by J. Clyde Mitchell, 77–116. Manchester: Manchester University Press.

Ernst, Manfred. 1994. *Winds of Change: Rapidly Growing Religious Groups in the Pacific Islands.* Suva, Fuji: Pacific Conference of Churches.

Fa'aleava, Toeutu. 2003. *Fitafita: Samoan Landsmen in the United States Navy, 1900–1951.* PhD diss., University of California, Berkeley.

Fairburn-Dunlop, Peggy, and Gabrielle Makisi, eds. 2003. *Making Our Place: Growing Up PI in New Zealand.* Palmerston North: Dunmore Press.

Fardon, Richard, ed. 1990. *Localizing Strategies: Regional Traditions of Ethnographic Writing.* Edinburgh: Scottish Academic Press.

Firth, Raymond. 1976. "Conversion from Paganism to Christianity: The Tikopia Case." *Royal Anthropological Institute News* 14: 3–7.

Fleming, Robin. 1997. *The Common Purse: Income Sharing in New Zealand Families.* Auckland: Auckland University Press with Bridget Williams Books.

Fleras, Augie, and Jean Leonard Elliott. 1992. *The 'Nations Within': Aboriginal-State Relations in Canada, the United States, and New Zealand.* Toronto: Oxford University Press.

Fleras, Augie, and Paul Spoonley. 1999. *Recalling Aotearoa: Indigenous Politics and Ethnic Relations in New Zealand.* Auckland: Oxford University Press.

Foner, Nancy. 2005. *In a New Land: A Comparative View of Immigration.* New York: New York University Press.

Fortes, Meyer. 1949. *The Web of Kinship among the Tallensi.* London: Oxford University Press.

Franco, Robert, and Simeamativa Mageo Aga. 1997. "From Houses Without Walls to Vertical Villages: Samoan Housing Transformations." In *Home in the Islands: Housing and Social Change in the Pacific,* edited by Jan Rensel and Margaret Rodman, 175–193. Honolulu: University of Hawai`i Press.

Franklin, Marianne. 2003. "I Define My Own Identity: Pacific Articulations of 'Race' and 'Culture' on the Internet." *Ethnicities* 3(4): 465–490.

———. 2004. *Postcolonial Politics, The Internet, and Everyday Life: Pacific Traversals Online.* London: Routledge.

Gailey, Christine Ward. 1991. "A Good Man Is Hard to Find: Overseas Migration and the Decentered Family in the Tongan Islands." *Critique of Anthropology* 12(1): 47–74.

Gershon, Ilana. 2005. Seeing Like a System: Luhmann for Anthropologists." *Anthropological Theory* 5(2): 99–116.

———. 2011. "Neoliberal Agency." *Current Anthropology* 52(4): 537–555.

Giddens, Anthony. 1984. *The Constitution of Society: Outline of the Theory of Structuration.* Cambridge: Polity Press.

Goddard, Michael. 2000. "Of Cabbages and Kin: The Value of an Analytic Distinction between Gifts and Commodities." *Critique of Anthropology* 20(2): 137–151.

Goldsmith, Michael. 2003. "Culture For and Against: Patterns of 'Culturespeak' in New Zealand." *Journal of the Polynesian Society* 112(3): 280–294.

Gordon, Tamar. 1990. "Inventing the Mormon Tongan Family." In *Christianity in Oceania: Ethnographic Perspectives,* edited by John Barker, 197–219. Lanham, MD: University Press of America.

Goss, Jon, and Bruce Lindquist. 2000. "Placing Movers: An Overview of the Asian-Pacific Migration System." *The Contemporary Pacific* 12(2): 385–414.

Graeber, David. 1996. "Beads and Money: Notes toward a Theory of Wealth and Power." *American Ethnologist* 23(1): 4–24.

Greenhouse, Carol, ed., with Roshanak Kheshti. 1998. *Democracy and Ethnography: Constructing Identities in Multicultural Liberal States.* Albany: State University of New York.

———. 2010. *Ethnographies of Neoliberalism*. Philadelphia: University of Pennsylvania Press.

Gregory, Chris. 1982. *Gifts and Commodities*. London: Academic Press.

Gregory, Robert J. 1993. "The Culture Broker Role: Ideas from Rehabilitation Models." *Adult Education and Development* 40: 71–75.

Gupta, Akhil, and James Ferguson. 1992. "Beyond 'Culture': Space, Identity, and the Politics of Difference." *Cultural Anthropology* 7(1): 6–23.

Hale, Charles R. 2005. "Neoliberal Multiculturalism: The Remaking of Cultural Rights and Racial Dominance in Central America." *PoLAR* 28(1): 10–19.

Hall, Kathleen. 2002. *Lives in Translation: Sikh Youth as British Citizens*. Philadelphia: University of Pennsylvania Press.

———. 2004. "The Ethnography of Imagined Communities: The Cultural Production of Sikh Ethnicity in Britain." *Annals of the American Academy of Political and Social Science* 595(1): 108–121.

Handler, Richard. 1988. *Nationalism and the Politics of Culture in Quebec*. Madison: University of Wisconsin Press.

Harding, Susan. 2000. *The Book of Jerry Falwell: Fundamentalist Language and Politics*. Princeton, NJ: Princeton University Press.

Harris, Mark, ed. 2007. *Ways of Knowing: New Approaches in the Anthropology of Experience and Learning*. Oxford: Berghahn Books.

Harvey, David. 2005. *Brief History of Neoliberalism*. Oxford: Oxford University Press.

Hau'ofa, Epeli. 1994. "Our Sea of Islands." *The Contemporary Pacific* 6(1): 148–161.

———. 1998. "The Ocean in Us." *The Contemporary Pacific* 10(2): 392–410.

Hefner, Robert, ed. 1993. *Conversion to Christianity: Historical and Anthropological Perspectives on a Great Transformation*. Berkeley: University of California Press.

Heller, Dieter. 2005. "Let It Flow: Economy, Spirituality, and Gender in the Sindhi Network." *Anthropological Theory* 5(2): 154–175.

Hereniko, Vilsoni. 2000. "Indigenous Knowledge and Academic Imperialism." In *Remembrance of Pacific Pasts: An Invitation to Remake History,* edited by Robert Borofsky, 78–91. Honolulu: University of Hawai'i Press.

Herzfeld, Michael. 1992. *The Social Production of Indifference: Exploring the Symbolic Roots of Western Bureaucracy*. New York: Berg.

Hess, Jim, Karen Nero, and Michael Burton. 2001. "Creating Options: Forming a Marshallese Community in Orange County, California." *The Contemporary Pacific* 13(1): 89–121.

Hill, Richard S. 2010. "Fitting Multiculturalism into Biculturalism: Māori-Pasifika Relations in New Zealand from the 1960s." *Ethnohistory* 57(2): 291–319.

Hing, Bill Ong. 1993. *Making and Remaking Asian America through Immigration Policy, 1850–1990*. Stanford, CA: Stanford University Press.

Hutchinson, Sharon. 1996. *Nuer Dilemmas: Coping with Money, War, and the State*. Berkeley: University of California Press.

James, Kerry. 1997. "Reading the Leaves: The Role of Tongan Women's Traditional Wealth and Other 'Contraflows' in the Processes of Modern Migration and Remittance." *Pacific Studies* 20(1): 1–27.

Janes, Craig. 1990. *Migration, Social Change, and Health: A Samoan Community in Urban California.* Stanford, CA: Stanford University Press.

Jezewski, Mary Ann. 1995. "Evolution of a Grounded Theory: Conflict Resolution through Culture Brokering." *Advances in Nursing Science* 17(3): 14–30.

Jezewski, Mary Ann, and Paula Sotnik. 2001. *The Rehabilitation Service Provider as Culture Broker.* Buffalo, NY: Center for International Rehabilitation Research Information and Exchange.

Jones, Alison. 1991. *"At School I've Got a Chance" Culture/Privilege: Pacific Islands and Pakeha Girls at School.* Palmerston North: Dunmore Press.

Jules-Rosette, Bennetta. 1975. "The Conversion Experience: The Apostles of John Maranke." *Journal of Religion in Africa.* 7(2): 132–164.

Ka'ili, Tevita O. 2005. "Tauhi va: Nurturing Tongan Sociospatial Ties in Maui and Beyond." *The Contemporary Pacific* 17(1): 83–114.

Kallen, Evelyn. 1982. *The Western Samoan Kinship Bridge: A Study in Migration, Social Change and the New Ethnicity.* Leiden: E. J. Brill.

Kapchan, Deborah. 2003. "Translating Folk Theories of Translation." In *Translating Cultures: Perspectives on Translation and Anthropology,* edited by Paula G. Rubel and Abraham Rosman, 135–152. New York: Berg.

Kauanui, J. Kehaulani. 1997. "Off-Island Hawai'ians 'Making Ourselves at 'Home': A (Gendered) Contradiction." *Women's Studies International Forum* 21(6): 681–693.

Keane, Webb. 2001. "Money Is No Object: Materiality, Desire, and Modernity in an Indonesian Society." In *The Empire of Things: Regimes of Value and Material Culture,* edited by Fred R. Myers, 65–90. Santa Fe, NM: School of American Research Press.

Kelly, John. 1995. "Diaspora and World War, Blood and Nation in Fiji and Hawai`i." *Public Culture* 7(3): 475–497.

Kelsey, Jane. 1995. *New Zealand Experiment: A World Model for Structural Adjustment?* Auckland: University of Auckland Press.

Lakoff, Robin. 2000. *Language War.* Berkeley: University of California Press.

Lange, Raeburn. 1997. *The Origins of the Christian Ministry in the Cook Islands and Samoa.* Christchurch, NZ: Macmillan Brown Centre for Pacific Studies.

Latour, Bruno. 1983. "Give Me a *Laboratory* and I Will *Raise* the World." In *Science Observed: Perspectives on the Social Study of Science,* edited by Karin Knorr-Cetina and Michael Joseph Mulkay, 141–170. London: Sage Publications.

——. 1999. *Pandora's Hope: Essays on the Reality of Science Studies.* Cambridge, MA: Harvard University Press.

Law, John. 1999. "After ANT: Complexity, Naming, and Topology." In *Actor Network Theory and After,* edited by John Law and John Hassard, 1–15. London: Blackwell.

Lee, Helen Morton. 2003. *Tongans Overseas: Between Two Shores.* Honolulu: University of Hawai`i Press.

Levine, Hal. 2003. "Some Reflections on Samoan Cultural Practice and Group Identity in Contemporary Wellington, New Zealand." *Journal of Intercultural Studies* 24(2): 175–186.

Lewthwaite, Gordon R., Christiane Mainzer, and Patrick J. Holland. 1973. "From Polynesia to California: Samoan Migration and Its Sequel." *Journal of Pacific History* 8: 133–157.

Lieber, Michael D., ed. 1977. *Exiles and Migrants in Oceania.* Honolulu: University of Hawai`i Press.

Lilomaiava-Doktor, Sa'iliemanu. 2009a. "Beyond "Migration": Samoan Population Movement (*Malaga*) and the Geography of Social Space (*Vā*)." *The Contemporary Pacific* 21(1): 1–32.

——. 2009b. "Samoan Transnationalism: Cultivating 'Home' and 'Reach.'" In *Migration and Transnationalism: Pacific Perspectives,* edited by Helen Lee and Steve Tupai Francis, 57–72. Canberra: The Australian National University E Press.

Linnekin, Jocelyn. 1991. "Fine Mats and Money: Contending Exchange Paradigms in Colonial Samoa." *Anthropological Quarterly* 64(1): 1–13.

Linnekin, Jocelyn, and Lin Poyer, eds. 1990. *Cultural Identity and Ethnicity in the Pacific.* Honolulu: University of Hawai`i Press.

Loomis, Terence. 1990. *Pacific Migrant Labour, Class, and Racism in New Zealand: Fresh Off the Boat.* Brookfield, VT: Gower Publishing.

Loury, Glenn C., Tariq Modood, and Steven M. Teles, eds. 2005. *Ethnicity, Social Mobility, and Public Policy: Comparing the USA and UK.* Cambridge: Cambridge University Press.

Lowe, Lisa. 1996. *Immigrant Acts: On Asian American Cultural Politics.* Durham: Duke University Press.

Lucy, John. 1999. "Reflexivity." *Journal of Linguistic Anthropology* 9(1–2): 212–215.

Luhmann, Niklas. 1990. *Essays on Self-Reference.* New York: Columbia University.

——. 1995. *Social Systems.* Translated by John Bednarz, Jr., with Dirk Baecker. Stanford, CA: Stanford University Press.

Mackey, Eva. 1999. *The House of Difference: Cultural Politics and National Identity in Canada.* London: Routledge.

Macpherson, Cluny. 1978. "The Polynesian Migrant Family: A Samoan Case Study." In *Families in New Zealand Society,* edited by Peggy Koopman-Boyden, 120–37. Wellington: Methuen Publications Ltd.

——. 1985. "Public and Private Views of Home." *Pacific Viewpoint* 26(1): 242–262.

——. 1992. "Economic and Political Restructuring and the Sustainability of Migrant Remittances: The Case of Western Samoa." *The Contemporary Pacific* 4(1): 109–135.

——. 1993. "Changing Patterns of Commitment for Island Homelands: A Case Study of Western Samoa." *Pacific Studies* 17(3): 83–116.

——. 1997a. "The Polynesian Diaspora: Communities and New Questions." In *Contemporary Migration in Oceania: Diaspora and Network.* Edited by Ken'ighi Sudo and Shuji Yoshida, 77–100. Osaka: Japan Centre for Area Studies, National Museum of Ethnology.

——. 1997b. "A Samoan Solution to the Limitations of Urban Housing in New Zealand." In *Home in the Islands: Housing and Social Change in the Pacific,* edited by Jan Rensel and Margaret Rodman, 151–174. Honolulu: University of Hawai`i Press.

——. 1999. "Changing Contours of Kinship: The Impacts of Social and Economic Development on Kinship Organization in the South Pacific." *Pacific Studies* 22(2): 71–96.

———. 2000. "Pacific Islanders." *Asia Pacific Viewpoint.* 42(1): 27–33.

Macpherson, Cluny, and La'avasa Macpherson. 2001. "Evangelical Religion among Pacific Island Migrants: New Faiths or Brief Diversions?" *Journal of Ritual Studies* 15(2): 27–37.

———. 2009. "Kinship and Transnationalism." In *Migration and Transnationalism: Pacific Perspectives,* edited by Helen Lee and Steve Tupai Francis, 73–90. Canberra: The Australian National University E Press.

Macpherson, Cluny, Bradd Shore, and Robert Franco, eds. 1978. *New Neighbors: Islanders in Adaptation.* Santa Cruz: Center for South Pacific Studies, University of California.

Mageo, Jeanette. 1989. "Aga, Amio, and Loto: Perspectives on the Structure of the Self in Samoa." *Oceania* 59(3): 181–201.

———. 1991. "Samoan Moral Discourse and the Loto." *American Anthropologist* 93: 405–420.

———. 1995. "The Reconfiguring Self." *American Anthropologist* 97: 282–296.

———. 1998. *Theorizing Self in Samoa: Emotions, Genders, and Sexualities.* Ann Arbor: University of Michigan Press.

Marcus, George. 1993. "Tonga's Contemporary Globalizing Strategies: Trading on Sovereignty amidst International Migration." In *Contemporary Pacific Societies: Studies in Development and Change,* edited by Victoria S. Lockwood, Thomas G. Harding, and Ben J. Wallace, 21–33. Englewood Cliffs, NJ: Prentice-Hall.

Marshall, Mac. 2004. *Namoluk beyond the Reef: The Transformation of a Micronesian Community.* Boulder, CO: Westview Press.

Marx, Karl. 1976 (1867). *Capital.* New York: Penguin Books.

Maurer, Bill. 1999. "Forget Locke? From Proprietor to Risk-Bearer in New Logics of Finance." *Public Culture* 11: 365–385.

Mauss, Marcel. 1954. *The Gift: The Form and Reason for Exchange in Archaic Societies.* New York: W. W. Norton.

Mayer, Philip. 1961a. "Migrancy and the Study of Africans in Town." *American Anthropologist* 64(3): 576–592.

———. 1961b. *Townsmen or Tribesmen: Conservatism and the Process of Urbanization in a South African City.* Capetown: Oxford University Press.

McGrath, Barbara. 2002. "Seattle Fa'a Samoa." *The Contemporary Pacific* 14(2): 307–340.

Meleisea, Malama. 1987a. *Lagaga: A Short History of Western Samoa.* Suva, Fiji: Institute of Pacific Studies of the University of the South Pacific.

———. 1987b. *The Making of Modern Samoa: Traditional Authority and Colonial Administration in the History of Western Samoa.* Suva, Fiji: Institute of Pacific Studies of the University of the South Pacific.

———. 1995. "To Whom Gods and Men Crowded." In *Tonga and Samoa: Images of Gender and Polity,* edited by Judith Huntsman, 19–36. Christchurch, NZ: Macmillan Brown Centre for Pacific Studies.

Milford, Sereisa. 1985–86. "Imperialism and Samoan National Identity." *Amerasia Journal* 12(1): 49–56.

Mills, C. Wright. 1959. *The Sociological Imagination.* Oxford: Oxford University Press.

Miyazaki, Hiro. 2004. *The Method of Hope: Anthropology, Philosophy, and Fijian Knowledge.* Stanford, CA: Stanford University Press.

Moffatt, Ken. 1999. "Surveillance and Government of the Welfare Recipient." In *Reading Foucault for Social Work*, edited by Adrienne S. Chambon, Allan Irving, and Laura Epstein, 219–246. New York: Columbia University Press.

Mulitalo-Lauta, Pa'a Tafaogalupe. 2000. *Fa'asamoa and Social Work within the New Zealand Context.* Palmerston North: Dunmore Press.

Munn, Nancy. 1992. *The Fame of Gawa: A Symbolic Study of Value Transformation in a Massim (Papua New Guinea) Society.* Durham, NC: Duke University Press.

National Center for Cultural Competence. 2004. *Bridging the Cultural Divide in Health Care Settings: The Essential Role of Cultural Broker Programs.* Washington, DC: Georgetown University Center for Child and Human Development.

New Zealand Department of Statistics. 2006. *New Zealand Census of Population and Dwellings.* Wellington: NZ Department of Statistics.

Ochs, Elinor. 1986. "Variation and Error: A Sociolinguistic Approach to Language Acquisition in Samoa." In *The Crosslinguistic Study of Language Acquisition,* edited by Dan Isaac Slobin, 1: 783–838. Mahwah, NJ: Lawrence Erlbaum Associates.

———. 1988. *Culture and Language Development: Language Acquisition and Language Socialization in a Samoan Village.* Cambridge: Cambridge University Press.

Ochs, Elinor, and Bambi Schiefflin. 1994. "Language Acquisition and Socialization: Three Developmental Stories and Their Implications." In *Language, Culture, and Society,* edited by Ben Blount, 470–512. New York: Waveland Press.

O'Malley, Pat. 1996. "Risk and Responsibility." In *Foucault and Political Reason: Liberalism, Neo-Liberalism, and Rationalities of Government,* edited by Andrew Barry, Thomas Osborne, and Nikolas Rose, 189–208. Chicago: University of Chicago Press.

Omi, Michael. 1999. "Racial Identity and the State: Contesting the Federal Standards for Classification." In *Race, Ethnicity, and Nationality in the United States toward the Twenty-First Century,* edited by Paul Wong, 25–33. Boulder, CO: Westview Press.

Omi, Michael, and Howard Winant. 1994. *Racial Formation in the United States: From the 1960s to the 1990s.* New York: Routledge.

Ong, Aihwa. 2003. *Buddha Is Hiding: Refugees, Citizenship, the New America.* Berkeley: University of California Press.

Orange, Claudia. 1987. *The Treaty of Waitangi.* Auckland: Allen and Unwin.

Orta, Andrew. 2004. "The Promise of Particularism and the Theology of Culture: Limits and Lessons of 'Neo-Boasianism'." *American Anthropologist* 106(3): 473–487.

Parnell, Phil. 2000. "The Innovations of Violent Days: Ignorance and the Regendering of Power in the Philippines." *Social Analysis* 44(2): 15–29.

Parry, Jonathan, and Maurice Bloch, eds. 1989. *Money and the Morality of Exchange,* Cambridge: Cambridge University Press.

Pearson, David. 1990. *A Dream Deferred: The Origins of Ethnic Conflict in New Zealand.* Wellington, NZ: Allen and Unwin.

Pitt, David C., and Cluny Macpherson. 1974. *Emerging Pluralism: Samoan Migrants in New Zealand.* Auckland: Longman Paul.

Portes, Alejandro, and Min Zhou. 1993. "The New Second Generation: Segmented Assimilation and Its Variants." *Annals of the American Academy of Political and Social Sciences* 530: 74–96.

Povinelli, Elizabeth. 2002. *The Cunning of Recognition: Indigenous Alterities and the Making of Australian Multiculturalism.* Durham, NC: Duke University Press.

Radhakrishnan, Rajagopalan. 1994. "Is the Ethnic 'Authentic' in the Diaspora?" In *The State of Asian America*, edited by K. Aguilar San Juan, 219–234. Boston: South End Press.

Raj, Dhooleka Sarhadi. 2003. *Where Are You From? Middle-class Migrants in the Modern World*. Berkeley: University of California Press.

Ramstad, Mette. 2000. *Conversion in the Pacific: Eastern Polynesian Latter-Day Saints' Conversion Accounts and Their Development of a LDS Identity*. PhD diss., University of Bergen.

Robbins, Joel. 2003. "On the Paradoxes of Global Pentacostalism and the Perils of Continuity Thinking." *Religion* 33(3): 221–231.

———. 2004. *Becoming Sinners: Christianity and Moral Torment in a Papua New Guinean Society*. Berkeley: University of California Press.

Rosen, Lawrence. 1995. *Other Intentions: Cultural Contexts and the Attribution of Inner States*. Santa Fe, NM: School of American Research Press.

Santiago-Irizarry, Vilma. 1996. "Culture as Cure." *Cultural Anthropology* 11(1): 3–24.

———. 2001. *Medicalizing Ethnicity: Constructing Latino Identity in a Psychiatric Setting*. Ithaca, NY: Cornell University Press.

Schoeffel, Penelope. 1978. "Gender, Status and Power in Samoa." *Canberra Anthropology* 1(2): 69–81.

———. 1999. "Samoan Exchange and 'Fine Mats': An Historical Reconsideration." *Journal of the Polynesian Society* 108(2): 117–148.

Scott, James. 1976. *The Moral Economy of the Peasant: Rebellion and Subsistence in Southeast Asia*. New Haven, CT: Yale University Press.

Shankman, Paul. 1993. "The Samoan Exodus." In *Contemporary Pacific Societies: Studies in Development and Change*, edited by Victoria Lockwood, Thomas Harding, and Ben Wallace, 156–170. Englewood Cliffs, NJ: Prentice Hall.

Shore, Bradd. 1976. "Adoptions, Alliance and Political Mobility in Samoa." In *Transactions in Kinship*, edited by Ivan Brady, 164–199. Honolulu: University of Hawai`i Press.

———. 1981. "Sexuality and Gender in Samoa: Conceptions and Missed Conceptions." In *Sexual Meanings: The Cultural Construction of Gender and Sexuality*, edited by Sherry Ortner and Harriet Whitehead, 192–215. Cambridge: Cambridge University Press.

———. 1982. *Sala'ilua: A Samoan Mystery*. New York: Columbia University Press.

Shukla, Sandhya. 2003. *India Abroad: Diasporic Cultures of Postwar America*. Princeton, NJ: Princeton University Press.

Small, Cathy. 1995. "The Birth and Growth of a Polynesian Women's Exchange Network." *Oceania* 65(3): 234–256.

———. 1997. *Voyages: From Tongan Villages to American Suburbs*. Ithaca, NY: Cornell University Press.

Spickard, Paul. 2002. "Pacific Islander Americans and Multiethnicity: A Vision of America's Future?" In *Pacific Diaspora: Island Peoples in the United States and Across the Pacific*, edited by Paul Spickard, Joanne Rondilla, and Debbie Hippolite Wright, 40–55. Honolulu: University of Hawai`i Press.

Spickard, Paul, Joanne Rondilla, and Debbie Hippolite Wright. 2002. *Pacific Diaspora: Island Peoples in the United States and Across the Pacific*. Honolulu: University of Hawai`i Press.

Star, Susan Leigh. 1999. "The Ethnography of Infrastructure." *American Behavioral Scientist* 43(3): 377–391.

St. Christian, Douglass. 1994. *Body/Work: Aspects of Embodiment in Western Samoa.* PhD diss., McMaster University.

Stillman, Amy. 2004. "Pacific-ing Asian Pacific American History." *Journal of Asian American Studies* 7(3): 241–270.

Strathern, Marilyn. 1991. *Partial Connections.* Savage, MD: Rowman & Littlefield.

——. 1995. "The Nice Thing About Culture Is That Everyone Has It." In *Shifting Contexts,* edited by Marilyn Strathern, 153–176. London: Routledge.

——. 1996. "Cutting the Network." *Journal of Royal Anthropological Institute* 2(3): 517–535.

Stromberg, Peter G. 1990. "Ideological Language in the Transformation of Identity." *American Anthropologist* 92(1): 42–56.

Tanielu, Lonise. 2000. "Education in Western Samoa: Reflections on My Experiences." In *Bitter Sweet: Indigenous Women in the Pacific,* edited by Alison Jones, Phyllis Herda, and Tamasailau M. Suaalii, 49–60. Dundein, NZ: University of Otago Press.

Taule'ale'ausumai, Feiloaiga. 1990. *The Word Made Flesh: Dissertation in Pastoral Theology.* PhD diss., University of Otago, Dundein, NZ.

Taussig, Michael. 1980. *The Devil and Commodity Fetishism in South America.* Chapel Hill: University of North Carolina Press.

Taylor, Janelle. 2003. "Confronting 'Culture' in Medicine's 'Culture of No Culture.'" *Academic Medicine* 78(6): 555–559.

Tcherkézoff, Serge. 1993. "The Illusion of Dualism in Samoa: 'Brothers-and-Sisters' Are Not 'Men-and-Women'." In *Gendered Anthropology,* edited by Teresa del Valle, 54–87. London: Routledge.

——. 1998. "Is Aristocracy Good for Democracy? A Contemporary Debate in Western Samoa." In *Pacific Answers to Western Hegemony: Cultural Practices of Identity Construction,* edited by Jürg Wassmann, 417–434. London: Berg.

——. 2000. "Are the Matai 'Out of Time'? Tradition and Democracy: Contemporary Ambiguities and Historical Transformations of the Concept of Chief." In *Governance in Samoa: Pulega i Samoa,* edited by Elise Huffer and Asofou So'o, 113–131. Canberra: Asia Pacific Press.

Teaiwa, Teresia. 2005a. "On Analogies: Rethinking the Pacific in a Global Context." *The Contemporary Pacific* 18(1): 71–87.

——. 2005b. "Native Thoughts: A Pacific Studies Take on Cultural Studies and Diaspora." In *Indigenous Diasporas and Dislocations,* edited by Graham Harvey and Charles D. Thompson Jr., 15–36. London: Ashgate.

Teaiwa, Teresia, and Sean Mallon. 2005. "Ambivalent Kinships? Pacific People in New Zealand." In *New Zealand Identities: Departures and Destinations,* edited by James H. Liu et al., 207–229. Wellington: Victoria University Press.

Tengan, Ty, and Geoff White. 2001. "Disappearing Worlds: Anthropology and Cultural Studies in Hawai`i and the Pacific." *The Contemporary Pacific* 13(2): 381–416.

Thaman, Konai Helu. 1985. "The Defining Distance: People, Places, and Worldview." In *Mobility and Identity in the Island Pacific,* edited by Murray Chapman, special issue of *Pacific Viewpoint* 26(1): 106–115.

Thompson, E. P. 1971. "The Moral Economy of the English Crowd in the Eighteenth Century." *Past and Present* 50: 76–136.

———. 1991. *Customs in Common.* New York: The New Press.

Tiatia, Jemaima. 1998. *Caught Between Two Cultures: A New Zealand Pacific Island Perspective.* Auckland: Christian Research Association.

Tomlinson, Matt. 2009. *In God's Image: The Metaculture of Fijian Christianity.* Berkeley: University of California Press.

Tsing, Anna. 2005. *Friction: An Ethnography of Global Connection.* Princeton, NJ: Princeton University Press.

Tuimaleali'ifano, Morgan. 1990. *Samoans in Fiji: Migration, Identity, and Communication.* Suva, Fiji: Institute of Pacific Studies of the University of the South Pacific.

Tupuola, Anne-Marie. 2004. "Pasifika Edgewalkers: Complicating the Achieved Identity Status in Youth Research." *Journal of Intercultural Studies* 25(1): 87–100.

Turner, Edith, with William Blodgett, Singleton Kahona, and Fideli Benwa. 1992. *Experiencing Ritual: A New Interpretation of African Healing.* Philadelphia: University of Pennsylvania Press.

Urciuoli, Bonnie. 1996. *Exposing Prejudice: Puerto Rican Experiences of Language, Race, and Class.* Boulder, CO: Westview Press.

———. 2003. "Excellence, Leadership, Skills, Diversity: Marketing Liberal Arts Education." *Language and Communication* 23: 385–408.

U.S. Census of Population and Housing. 2000. *Summary Population and Housing Characteristics: United States.* Washington: Government Printing Office.

Va'a, Leulu Felise. 2001. *Saili Matagi: Samoan Migrants in Australia.* Suva, Fiji: Institute of Pacific Studies of the University of the South Pacific.

Van de Port, Mattijs. 1999. "'It Takes a Serb to Know a Serb': Uncovering the Roots of 'Obstinate Otherness' in Serbia." *Critique of Anthropology* 19(1): 7–30.

Vasta, Ellie. 2004. "Community, the State, and the Deserving Citizen: Pacific Islanders in Australia." *Journal of Ethnic and Migration Studies* 30(1): 195–213.

Vete, Mele. 1995. "The Determinants of Remittances among Tongans in Auckland." *Asian and Pacific Migration Journal* 4(1): 55–68.

Wagner, Roy. 1981. *The Invention of Culture.* Chicago: University of Chicago Press.

———. 1995. "Hazarding Intent: Why Sogo Left Hweabi." In *Other Intentions: Cultural Contexts and the Attribution of Inner States,* edited by Lawrence Rosen, 163–176. Santa Fe, NM: School of American Research Press.

Williams, Brackette. 1989. "A Class Act: Anthropology and the Race to Nation across Ethnic Terrain." *Annual Review of Anthropology* 18: 401–444.

Yamamoto, Matori. 1997. "Samoan Diaspora and Ceremonial Exchange." In *Population Movement in the Modern World/Contemporary Migration in Oceania: Diaspora and Network.* JCAS Symposium Series no. 3. Osaka: Japan Center for Area Studies.

Yanagisako, Sylvia, and Carol Delaney, eds. 1995. *Naturalizing Power: Essays in Feminist Cultural Analysis.* New York: Routledge.

Yengoyan, Aram A. 1986. "Theory in Anthropology: On the Demise of the Concept of Culture." *Comparative Studies in Society and History* 28(2): 368–374.

Žižek, Slavoj. 1989. *The Sublime Object of Ideology.* New York: Verso.

Index

St. Christian, Douglass, 17n8, 120, 151–52
strategically deployed shifters, 124, 126
Strathern, Marilyn, 128, 130
Stromberg, Peter, 67
systems
    cultural mediators in, 96–105, 110, 111–13
    families as, 106–10
    reflexivity in, 89–92, 94, 104–10
    solipsistic aspect of, 105, 109
    system-carriers, 92–93, 94–95, 101, 108, 109, 113
    term, 95
    See also bureaucracies

Tangata Whenua (people of the land), 81
"The Task of the Translator" (Benjamin), 100
Taussig, Michael, 33
Thompson, E. P., 57n5
Tizard, Judith, 128
translators, 94, 95, 96, 99–102, 103–4, 111–13
Treaty of Waitangi, 80, 81, 82–83
Tuiasosopo, Nofoaluma, 2–3
tulafale (talking chiefs), 36
Turner, Edith, 55
Turner, Victor, 55

United States
    assimilation in, 138–39, 140
    census in, 79, 86, 154
    children and youth in, 20, 143
    cultural differences in, 74–75
    cultural expertise in, 144–45, 149–50
    culture-bearers in, 165–66

ethnicity and race in, 86, 87, 165–66
and fine mats, 59
fundable classifications in, 83–87
motives for migration to, 45
multiculturalism in, 77–79, 77n1
neoliberalism in, 11, 166
relationship with Samoa, 8–9
ritual exchanges (*fa'alavelave*) in, 60
Samoan population in, 8, 10, 83
separation of church and state in, 84–85
and slavery, 77
social services in, 72–76, 114
welfare-to-work legislation in, 11, 75, 114, 152
Urciuoli, Bonnie, 86, 124

values, 101
Van de Port, Mattijs, 100n4

Wagner, Roy, 14n6
weddings, 35–36, 37, 58
welfare benefits, 43n11
Western Samoa, 8. *See also* Samoa
white, desire or attempt to be, 145, 147–48, 162
Williams, Brackette, 5, 78
Williams, John, 49, 75
wives, 118–19
women, 85, 118–19

Yamamoto, Matori, 34
Young, V. S., 131
youth. *See* children and youth